# SAILING AROUND BRITAIN

# SAILING AROUND BRITAIN

## A Weekend Sailor's Voyage in 50 Day Sails

KIM C. STURGESS

FERNHURST
BOOKS

This edition first published in 2015 by Fernhurst Books Limited
62 Brandon Parade, Holly Walk, Leamington Spa, Warwickshire, CV32 4JE, UK
Tel: +44 (0) 1926 337488 | www.fernhurstbooks.com



This content originally published as "This Precious Isle" by Matador, an imprint of Troubador Publishing Ltd.



British Library Cataloguing in Publication Data
A catalogue record for this book is available from the British Library
ISBN 978-1-909911-17-8

Cover design by Rachel Atkins
Cover photography by Kim C. Sturgess and Heather Criggie
Typeset in 12pt Galliard BT by Troubador Publishing Ltd, Leicester, UK
Printed in China through World Print

*For everyone on the Jubilee Line*

*Contents*

*Acknowledgements*

I offer my profound thanks to Tanya Apel for lending me Hobo to make the cruise. I also thank crew members Heather Criggie, Jim Guckian, Phil Lloyd, Terry Naude, Anders Ovegård, and Rebecca Scott. Sincere thanks also to my two caring watchers, Terry F. Insull and Mary Sturgess.

Editors: Paula G. McGrath and Heather Criggie.

*List of Stopovers*

| | | |
|---|---|---|
| 1 | Greenwich | London |
| 2 | Burnham -on-Crouch | Essex |
| 3 | Harwich | Essex |
| 4 | Lowestoft | Suffolk |
| 5 | Grimsby | NE Lincolnshire |
| 6 | Filey Bay | N Yorkshire |
| 7 | Scarborough | N Yorkshire |
| 8 | Hartlepool | Hartlepool |
| 9 | Amble | Northumberland |
| 10 | Eyemouth | Borders |
| 11 | Abroath | Angus |
| 12 | Aberdeen | Aberdeen |
| 13 | Peterhead | Aberdeen |
| 14 | Buckie | Moray |
| 15 | Inverness | Highlands |
| 16 | Loch Ness | Highlands |
| 17 | Corpach | Highlands |
| 18 | Oban | Highlands |
| 19 | Tobermory | Argyll and Bute |
| 20 | Craobh Haven | Argyll and Bute |
| 21 | Cairnbaan | Argyll and Bute |
| 22 | Tarbert | Argyll and Bute |
| 23 | Rothesay | Argyll and Bute |
| 24 | Inverkip | Inverclyde |
| 25 | Troon | South Ayrshire |
| 26 | Stranraer | Dumfries and Galloway |
| 27 | Bangor | County Down |
| 28 | Ardglass | County Down |
| 29 | Dún Laoghaire | Dún Laoghaire-Rathdown |
| 30 | Arklow | County Wexford |
| 31 | Rosslare | County Wexford |
| 32 | Kilmore Quay | County Wicklow |
| 33 | Milford Haven | Pembrokeshire |
| 34 | Padstow | Cornwall |
| 35 | Newlyn | Cornwall |
| 36 | Falmouth | Cornwall |
| 37 | Plymouth | Devon |
| 38 | Dartmouth | Devon |
| 39 | Poole | Dorset |
| 40 | Lymington | Hampshire |
| 41 | Gosport | Hampshire |
| 42 | Brighton | East Sussex |
| 43 | Eastbourne | East Sussex |
| 44 | Dover | Kent |
| 45 | Ramsgate | Kent |
| 46 | Chatham | Kent |

*Map of the route around Britain and Ireland*

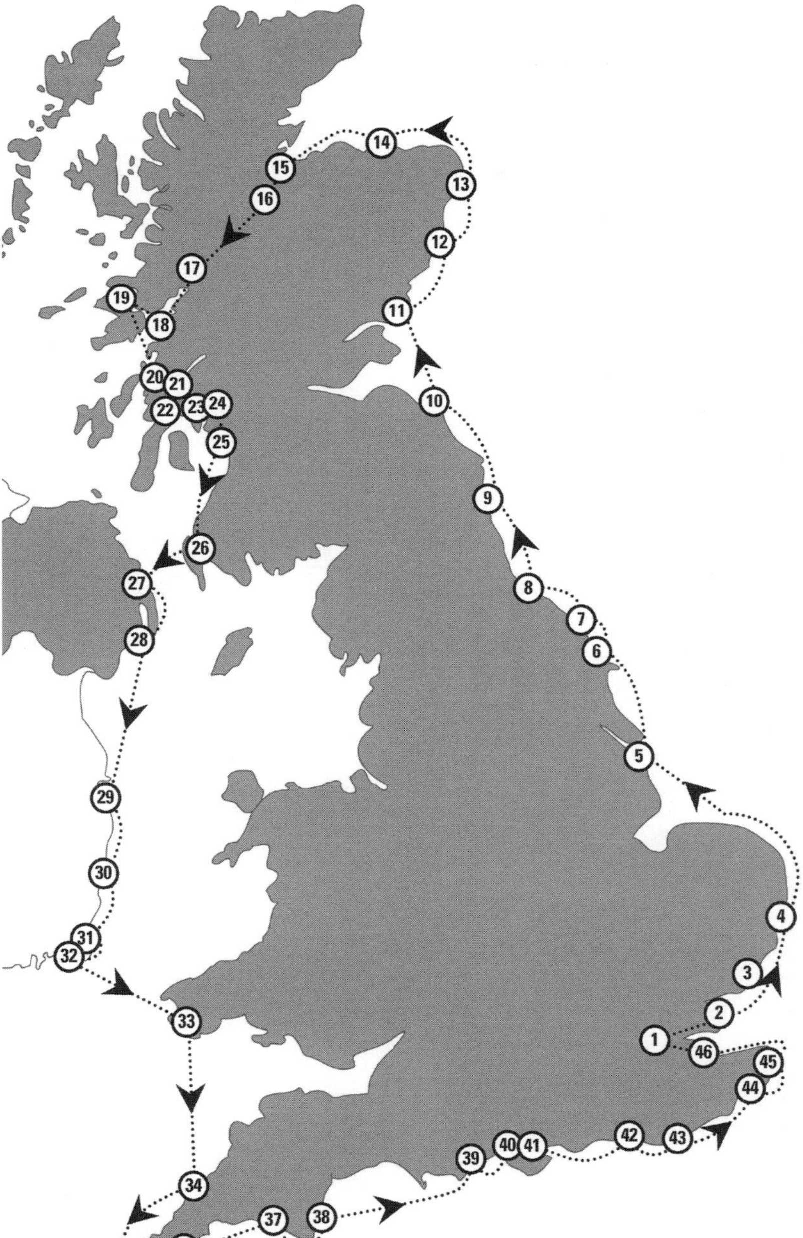

# *Preface*

Why would anyone wish to sail around Britain? My answer to the question is quite simple – to prove to oneself you can do it and to see what Shakespeare called this 'scepter'd isle'. Either reason would be enough to justify casually fantasising the trip in the yacht club bar or perhaps while commuting to work on the morning train, but to actually set out on the adventure takes a good deal of bravery. Not bravery of the kind that flowed in the veins of the yeoman Tudor and Elizabethan sailors, who set out from here to sail where the chart makers only guessed at the coastlines and distances, but the bravery of forsaking the comfort of the bed, sofa and passive TV entertainment. Braving the scorn of friends and family who question and suggest sailing around Britain is an unpleasant, if not foolish, idea for an urbanised fifty-year-old.

While many leisure sailors dream of long-term cruising around the sun warmed Mediterranean or possibly even crossing the Atlantic before perhaps setting off around the world, the far more logical starting point to adventure is nearer to home. Before tackling all the challenging aspects of "foreign" seas something more domestic can be achieved. I believe, rather than setting off for exotic sounding destinations, sailing around Britain is the better voyage for any competent sailor with free time. We Britons are lucky to live on an island and the need for a challenging cruising destination is well met by the concept of home to home via the ports of the four British nations made five, perhaps, by the addition of that emerald Republic.

The catalyst for my own around Britain adventure was a couple of small media stories from the autumn and winter of 2006. Firstly, there was Katie Miller, the eighteen-year-old who sailed solo around Britain in her little 21 foot Corribee, and then fourteen-year-old Michael Perham's brave, but bizarre, solo project of sailing across the Atlantic, shadowed closely by his father in an identical yacht. To me, a fifty-year-old male with leisure time on his hands, but perhaps not so much left of his 'threescore and ten', it seemed as if children were making voyages I had never even seriously considered. And, of course, in this there lurked a kind of subliminal challenge. If teenagers could do it, surely I could? I had no need to foolishly imagine myself as equal to the great Ernest Shackleton or Robin Knox-Johnston but just think of "little" Katie and Michael. I began to hunger to sail the home waters that somehow felt local and mine. So as I enjoyed Christmas 2006 on a relaxed, for the over-fifties Saga holiday in Rome, I pondered setting out on a real adventure. It was to be sailing around Britain visiting the coastline of my home island, and it would be as soon as possible, namely summer of 2007.

Yet, naturally, there were issues I needed to resolve. Firstly I didn't have a boat suitable for a cruise of this kind and, secondly, and perhaps more importantly, exactly what kind of cruise was this going to be? Just how far was it around Britain? I needed to do some research – and quickly. I hunted on the internet, checked the book shops and visited the library at the Cruising Association. While there were several books complete with colourful descriptions of puffins, dolphins, sunrises and cooking casseroles, I wanted the type of information that would allow me, as a first time voyager, to quantify the task ahead. Could I circumnavigate without a crew of rum swilling, salt water hardened masochists and, how long would it take? Sadly for me, in May 2007, there wasn't a single book available to provide the answers I needed. This publishing anomaly was rectified in 2008 – too late for me – and at the time of writing there are now two excellent volumes in print.

Without the pilot book I needed, I was a frustrated adventurer from metropolitan Wapping, but very keen to start my voyage. So without preparation or possessing a glossy "how to do it manual", perhaps, like my heroes the Elizabethan adventurers, I would have to sail "blind" and sail I did. Summer 2007 from the banks of the Thames, like so many adventurers before me I sailed out to the sea and then on around Britain.

# PART ONE

## SWAPPING THE LONDON UNDERGROUND FOR BRITISH SEAS

## Cruise Philosophy

To undertake a long cruise of this sort requires profound mental preparation as, with any adventure, it is the right mental approach that leads to success. Initially, when I contemplated sailing around Britain, I was ignorant as to the extent of the emotional challenge and the stamina needed to complete the trip. However, this very naïveté was in fact beneficial as it led me to formulate a philosophy that avoided the fear of the unknown, liberating me to let go of home and set sail. The philosophy I adopted was to regard the circumnavigation of the UK as just a series of linked day trips – as it turned out, fifty day trips.

I believe many people faced with the idea of sailing more than 1900 nautical miles (nm) and spending ninety-four days on board a yacht, would be prone to panic, or at the least feel very intimidated by the scale of the task ahead. Many people might worry and doubt their ability to sail the distance. I believe many people faced with a long 1900 nautical mile, ninety-four day cruise would in fact be put off by the thought and, therefore, choose to fail rather than even start.

However, my adopted philosophy of a series of linked day trips should, I believe, allow any competent sailor like me to be confident and to set sail. Every competent sailor can and does "day sail". Day sailing is undertaken every weekend by hundreds of thousands of sailors without extensive preparation or without fear and anxiety. My decision to philosophise my cruise around Britain as a series of linked day trips, each night being spent in port or at anchor, allowed me to feel very normal, not at all brave.

It is our very island geography that allows this approach.

Being an island with a population of more than sixty-two million people has ensured that all around our coast there are towns and communities with harbours and marinas. By simple passage planning, it is possible for a yacht to sail from harbour to harbour, removing the need to undertake huge offshore passages or even sail through the dark night. All my preparation, or rather my lack of preparation, resulted from adopting the linked day trip philosophy.

An additional benefit of this philosophy was that it allowed me to set sail in a "normal" yacht and with a moderate budget. Conversely, sailors without the day trip philosophy, believing he or she was embarking on a long 1900 nautical mile, ninety-four day voyage might need an exceptional yacht, extensively refitted with the best state of the art equipment money could buy. The sailor would also need to be a fearless adventurer, and someone prepared to undergo great hardships. Prior to embarkation, detailed calculations would need to be made to ensure enough water, food and fuel. Passage planning would require additional study and in-depth knowledge. Lastly, the "big trip" 1900 nautical mile sailor would have to leave family and friends, and trust his or her home to manage itself for the period of the voyage.

Using my linked day trip approach, none of the above drama is necessary. Any reasonably maintained yacht designed for coastal cruising will suffice. Food and fuel, indeed all supplies, can be obtained at any overnight harbour. Breakages or repairs can be attended to at leisure and as and when they occur, merely extending the number of nights spent in any particular harbour. Detailed passage planning can be undertaken just one or two days ahead. The linked day trip approach allows the average competent sailor to undertake and complete 1900 nautical miles without a personality bypass or the need to morph into a duplicate of celebrity superheroes Robin Knox-Johnston or Ellen MacArthur.

The linked day trip approach also allows the sailor to pause along the way without confronting the spectre of failure. Anywhere around the UK, should the need arise, a sailor can secure the yacht, board a train and return home to rest or to attend to pressing family affairs. Once the home crisis has been dealt with, the very same train returns the sailor to the awaiting yacht, and the cruise can continue. Naturally, I believe this option should, like a fire extinguisher, only be used in an emergency, but like a fire extinguisher it is comforting to know the option is there.

While I recommend this linked day trip philosophy over the more conventional major voyage approach, it is, of course, not totally free from drawbacks. Entering and exiting harbours and anchorages every evening can in some instances add considerable distance to the shortest route around Britain. Also, choosing to enter harbour each evening requires the sailor to study and use favourable tide far more than the sailor who chooses to make trips of say 48 hours or more. It is a fact that it takes longer to complete the circumnavigation by this linked day trip method. But then, this is a cruise for adventure and not a race, and I suggest for a sailor, time is merely a convenient way to report the rising and setting of the sun, the ebb and the flood of a tide.

Whilst I had formulated a philosophy for my cruise, empowering me and encouraging an early and carefree embarkation, I did however, need to decide what to do when I reached the mouth of the Thames. Would I turn left and go to the north or right, and go south? Turning left would mean the cruise would be anticlockwise around Britain whereas turning right would be clockwise. I chose anticlockwise.

Alone in my warm and comfy home, the decision seemed quite simple, although, later, during the voyage, after I was constantly challenged by interested enquirers as to why I chose this direction, I began to realise the more usual route was the other way. Apparently, several weeks spent in hard study of the prevailing sea currents around the British Isles will reveal to a student that clockwise might be the favoured direction. Study of wind direction is far less unequivocal although some might claim the prevailing southwesterly air flow, moving under the influence of the famed jet stream, again suggests a clockwise rounding.

However, when I made my decision for the anticlockwise route I was unaware of the twin theories concerning prevailing sea current or wind. To me Britain was an island and therefore, logically, if naively, I had to sail around it in a circle, so it didn't matter which way I went. My personal choice depended on just one key issue; namely where on the circle did I want to be in midsummer, or perhaps, more correctly, where didn't I want to be? Where I didn't want to be was anywhere around the Highlands of Scotland. Why? My answer is midges.

Scotland has many attractive features and I was excited by the prospect of, for the first time, enjoying the famous Lochs, the Highlands and the seafood. However, the infamous Highland biting midges, or to give them their scientific name, Culicoides Impunctatus, were something I wanted to avoid. I'm no Indiana Jones and flying, crawling or burrowing bugs are not for me. I hate getting bitten or forced to flee into a stuffy cabin the moment daylight starts to fade.

The facts about the Highland midge are these, from June to August this wee beastie plagues walkers, casual visitors and sailors or anyone silly enough to be in northern Scotland. From June onwards biblical swarms of midges –

that is females – are genetically disposed to feed on blood prior to laying their eggs. We, the unfortunate public, provide the blood donation. So bad are the biting midges that there is even an online internet midge forecast to allow visitors to assess just how badly they are going to suffer. That these midges prefer damp conditions and the Lochs and islands offer all the dampness any flying, would-be vampire might require, worried me.

So my decision was to ensure I avoided the Highlands in June, July and August. With this focused decision then made, its consequence was that I would need to travel anticlockwise thereby, potentially, I would be on the south coast of England in the "hottest" period of the summer. This seemed an attractive prospect and while at home in Wapping I fantasised about sunshine and sailing in shorts and I feared how I was going to keep the cabin cool at night. Quite how ridiculous this fear was only became apparent as I experienced the non-summer of 2007. The holiday conditions I rightfully deserved didn't materialise but by travelling anticlockwise I did succeed in avoiding the feared Highland biting midge.

In my opinion any competent weekend sailor could sail around the British Isles, as, with reasonable planning, very little of the cruise is particularly difficult. No section of the coast requires specialist knowledge and, a sailor competent enough to undertake a day trip of, say 50 nautical miles, could circumnavigate.

In my own case, I had just a Royal Yachting Association Day Skipper qualification. But in addition to this, and far more importantly, I had, for a number of years, sailed a variety of yachts both as crew and skipper. I had learned to sail at aged 24, while living in Doha, Qatar, long before it became famous for sponsoring sporting events or for its 5-star airline or being awarded the World Cup in 2022. Since I was to be there four years, I quickly decided I needed to take up a regular sport to help keep myself in mental health as for many, the expatriate lifestyle is only one step away from the padded cell. The choices available were rugby or sailing and I sensibly chose sailing. At the Doha Sailing Association I was taught to sail in their fleet of 470 Olympic class dinghies. Once a sailor, I became a racer. While at the time, I did greatly enjoy the club 470 and Laser dinghy racing on the warm turquoise gulf waters, I didn't realise that this was probably to be the best sailing of my life. But as I learned to race, I swallowed the sailing bug along with a lot of hot salt water. When I returned to Britain, I continued dinghy sailing until, finally, I decided boats that didn't capsize were far better for our climate.

My later sailing experience included the usual two week flotilla holiday in Greece and several trips crewing on a friend's yacht around Sweden's Baltic coast. During this twenty or so years sailing, prior to cruising around Britain, I logged about 5,800 nautical miles mostly in sight of the coast but with the occasional cross channel trip to France. While confident I could sail and navigate a 30 foot yacht in most weather conditions, I had never knowingly faced a full gale at sea.

If I was to categorise myself it would be as a fairly conservative "weekend" sailor with a passionate love of racing. The around Britain cruise was the first substantial voyage I attempted. To further clarify the extent of my sailing experience, prior to undertaking the British cruise, I had only sailed on the south coast of England. This meant from Gravesend on the Thames, all the way up to and down from Scotland, until I reached Plymouth in Devon, every bay, every headland and every harbour was, for me, a first time event.

The purpose of qualifying my sailing experience in this manner is to emphasise my belief that sailing around Britain is within the scope of most competent sailors. However, it is of course for each person to decide their own level of competency. Perhaps, as a self-test, a sailor could ask themselves one simple question:

> Would you feel capable of taking responsibility for the lives of your children or grandchildren while sailing 50 nautical miles at sea over a weekend?

If the answer to this important question is yes, I would suggest, probably, like me, you are capable of sailing around Britain.

## Hobo the Yacht

There are two central characters in this saga of adventure – the boat and me. This is the boat's story.

Originally when deciding on my cruise, I'd intended buying a 27 foot long, lightweight cruiser/racer for my adventure, a Rob Humphreys designed MGC 27. This is a class of boat I knew well since it was the type of yacht I first owned after giving up dinghy sailing. As well as personally approving its sailing characteristics, I wanted something easily handled by a solo sailor. The MGC 27 was designed to use a self-tacking jib and this system seemed ideal for coastal solo sailing. The size of boat was also just right. I am a lightweight male, in fact a 62 kilo, or if you prefer, a mere 10 stone. As muscle strength and body weight are closely related, I wanted a cruise boat where the loadings on sail halyards and sheets were minimised and thereby within my capability to haul, without me taking a long course of anabolic steroids.

However, things were not to work out the way I'd planned. I did find a likely yacht for sale, and agreed with the vendor a reasonable price, but unfortunately when the Surveyor's condition report on the 20 year old yacht was completed, it told of many hairline cracks around the base of the mast. As this was not what I wanted on a yacht about to make a 1900 nautical mile trip, the purchase fell through in February 2007.

Without a solid boat, big enough to make the trip, it appeared obvious that I would have to postpone my cruise. I was very frustrated and I wracked my brain trying to create solutions to the problem.

But then it came to me, what about borrowing a boat?

Surely with all the many thousands of boats sitting unused on moorings or in marinas, I could find one boat to borrow? Perhaps a foolish hope, but as I had a mere two months before my planned start date, I had nothing to lose except perhaps a few friends.

My starting point for the search was my own Greenwich Yacht Club on the Thames, and as I walked along the tow path towards the Millennium Dome, I studied the boats on the moorings. And there she was, Hobo, lying sedately to her warps, fringed in green weed, not having been off the mooring for several months.

Hobo is a Hanse 301 built in 2001 and at 30 feet, she was bigger and heavier than I originally intended for my largely solo adventure. She also had several less than attractive characteristics for a solo sailor, such as not having the self-tacking jib I prefer, or even a roller furling headsail. The engine, a Volvo 10 hp, was also a little underpowered for a 30 foot, 6173 lb displacement boat. But in all other aspects, she looked to me like a long legged, smooth skinned pert German supermodel – but without all the unpleasant vomiting and tantrums. I was very smitten, but would she fancy me?

A bit of internet research revealed that the Hanse 301 had suffered a troubled childhood after being born to the Swedish designer Carl Beyer in the 1980's and then marketed around the Baltic as the Aphrodite 29. When boat production in Sweden ceased, the hull mould found its way to the former East Germany. Here the boat remerged as, first, the fractional rigged Hanse 291, and then later, as the more powerful Hanse 301. A yacht with a racy profile and, like a certain Miss Schiffer, lots of sail area.

Hobo's owner responded positively to my very provocative phone call, and a meeting was speedily arranged at the club. To my great joy the loan of the boat was agreed.

It was almost too easy. But as the proverb suggests, "don't look a gift horse – or supermodel – in the mouth". The chance to borrow beautiful Hobo for three months was the type of "gift" I wasn't going to question. So after a very brief fifteen minute trial sail on the river it was all agreed. I was easily seduced and Hobo and I, like teenagers at an end of term party, rushed to bed together.

## Safety for a Sailor

Feelings about safety are a very personal matter. On a yacht at sea there is no health and safety officer – thank god – assessment of risk, and any response to it, is up to the individual. For millions of weekend sailors, being at sea is no more frightening than running down a flight of steps. For other people, however, sailing seems to be associated with the idea of injuring themselves and fear is so prominent in their emotional hierarchy that they shun the opportunity for excitement and adventure. In trying to stay safe they embrace a life of mundane repetition, believing, perhaps, that repeating what they have already done avoids risk.

So, for some people, the thought of the sea and a small yacht, a form of transport quite insignificant to the forces of nature, are a scary prospect and something unsafe and best avoided. Maybe they are right, but possibly a life of mundane repetition is not quite as safe as it might seem. For many Londoners the tube and bus bombings of 7th July 2005 reaffirmed what they already knew, but seldom voiced – repetition is not 100% safe. There are risks in going to work or college or just in going out to buy groceries. In London citizens rely on others to keep them safe or at least to reduce the risks. They are dependent on the Security Service, the Police, hospitals, bus drivers and legions of other good professionals – always nameless, usually remote and often wearing a uniform.

On a yacht it is different, as safety is very personal. Your safety depends on just you and perhaps your god. No one at sea is 100% safe, but then neither are the hundreds of thousands who commute on public transport to and from work each day. Unlike the commuter in London, sailors can, themselves, assess the risks and make decisions likely to minimise them. As to safety at sea the sailor is sovereign.

As I set off on my cruise I knew, as a solo sailor, the main risk to my life was me falling overboard and watching my yacht sail away. The fact is a fully dressed, solo sailor falling off a moving yacht, and then immersed in cold sea water, seldom manages to climb back aboard and is rarely rescued. A person's survival time after being thrown into the sea is dependent on many factors, their body weight – and here is one time when it is good to be fat – general fitness, and the wave conditions, as these can all affect survival. While there are many variables, so beloved by scientists, it is perhaps best to simply assume that a sailor falling overboard from a yacht will be close to death after 30 to 60 minutes. For any solo sailor, knowing that the UK Search and Rescue Service have a target time of 60 minutes to reach a casualty from first alert, is hardly reassuring, given that no one will know you are in the water. So the maxim is – don't fall off.

The various instruction manuals sold by the Royal Yachting Association, or leaflets given out by the Royal National Lifeboat Institute, all state clearly, and in bold type, that a sailor should always wear a life jacket and be tied to the yacht by a lifeline. Good advice, and very logical. Of course, to do so, does not guarantee 100% safety. A solo sailor in the water and tied to a yacht, can be dragged alongside the boat for many miles and unable to get back aboard. A solo sailor, not tied by lifeline but wearing a life jacket, may live 60 minutes, but it is highly unlikely any would-be rescuer would know that they needed help. So don't fall off.

My personal safety decision was always to wear a life jacket but seldom use a lifeline. I chose to adopt a standard climbing technique, namely that I would never let go of the boat with both hands at the same moment. I also spent considerable time on my knees, crawling along the deck, keeping my centre of gravity low, hoping that I could reduce the risk that I would over balance and plunge into the sea.

My other decision on matters related to major catastrophe, was with regard to a life raft. Hobo didn't have one. I've never crewed on a yacht "day-sailing" around the coast where the skipper provided a life raft. I assessed my risks and concluded that, as Hobo hadn't had a life raft when I borrowed her, she wouldn't have one for my cruise. I am aware that some sailors could regard my personal choice as a little cavalier. Naturally I disagree. To help justify my philosophy on life rafts I offer the reader this; since reaching the age of nineteen I've flown as a passenger on commercial aircraft probably once or twice a year and never have I, nor indeed, anyone else been offered a parachute. Lack of a parachute has never stopped me from flying.

As to other safety issues, I ensured I had plenty of good quality marine type clothing; a Helly Hansen underwear layer, Musto fibre pile mid-layer, and Henry Lloyd outer-layer, all crowned by a polar fleece hat. With this unflattering "haute couture" ensemble, even during the UK summer of 2007, I managed to stay tolerably tepid – to truly be warm I needed the sun, and in summer 2007, sun rarely managed to pierce the dense grey cloud. Before I left a harbour I ensured I had enough food prepared and ready to hand for constant consumption over the projected passage period. Forget balanced diets and long-term health concerns, when at sea, calories are needed to help the body stay "uncold" and the brain stay alert, however long the passage might take. Tiredness and cold when combined are much more dangerous to the sailor than high cholesterol or the wild sea. A tired and cold sailor, when faced with a problem or emergency, often makes the wrong decision.

The other key safety element within the remit of the solo sailor is adequate passage planning. Before leaving a harbour a smart sailor will have spent considerable time planning the route, studying the marine charts, calculating tides and predicting weather conditions over a twelve to eighteen hour period. Yes, easily written, but much harder to do. The passage plan is metaphorically either a treasure map or an epitaph. Done well it will "lead" the solo sailor to the next haven. Done badly – well just don't do it badly.

Within the plan there needs to be a "bolt-hole", an identified secondary destination, available to the yacht should the weather change or the primary haven prove to be too distant to reach. Planning for arrival is also important. Just how will you recognise the harbour entrance or anchorage? Will there be enough water under the keel to allow you to enter? Just where are the shoals or rocks that might wreck your yacht just as you start to relax and assume you are safe? All this needs to be devised and written down in a form that, even when tired, cold and possibly anxious (hopefully, if you have planned well there is no need to be frightened) you will still be able to understand. This is the ideal. Of course many times on my cruise I found my plan less than ideal.

Leaving harbour is the least dangerous part of a passage – it is on arrival that most mishaps occur. In my case, 90% of the arrivals were at a harbour or anchorage being visited for the first time in my life. After twelve or so hours at sea, tired, and often in a hurry, I would have to find an entrance I'd never seen before and navigate my way between hazards only made known to me by tiny symbols on a paper chart. As a solo sailor there is no smiling pilot, blue badge guide or hostess waving you towards the safe route. Therefore, you, alone, must spot and comprehend the land marks and, using your passage plan, make timely decisions. So passage planning needs to be comprehensive and enjoyed. You and your plan will be responsible for your safety. It is very personal.

While I chose to – had to – sail solo for much of my cruise, I utilised those persons sensibly, still on land to record my departures and arrivals. I figured, if I was to be lost a sea, I wanted someone on land to know approximately where to look for me. Each day before leaving harbour I would use my mobile phone to text my departure time and estimated time and point of arrival to those I could trust to care for my wellbeing – namely Mary, my former wife and a RYA Yachtmaster and Terry, my sister. I relied upon them to await my later text announcing my safe arrival. However tired or cold I never forgot to text my two watchers to confirm another day had ended safely.

There were other watchers scratching brief notes in pencil that served as a record of my whereabouts. Her Majesty's Coastguard listens on VHF marine radio for mariners at sea. My radio call to the appropriate designated Coastguard Station was usually answered by a friendly and professional voice, someone well used to recording the progress of seafarers undertaking passage far from land and the comfort of home. I would tell them my yacht's name and length, number of persons on board, destination and estimated arrival time. Just as with the text to my personal watchers, the Coastguard was always contacted on my safe arrival thereby ensuring no brave volunteers were put at risk making unnecessary checks as to my location.

Concepts of safety are both relative and personal. Safety at sea is a sailor's personal and exclusive responsibility. When you get it right, the feeling of satisfaction is immense. There can be no greater personal satisfaction than staying alive.

## *Weather in Summer 2007*

Fate had decreed the year of my adventure was to make the history books; not because of myself, or any of the other valiant mariners sailing around our island, but because of the weather. The newspaper headlines were to claim the months of May, June and July 2007 were the "wettest on record" or, alternatively, as stated by the Meteorological Office, "the worst summer since 1776" – this particular year, apparently, the first that an official with too much time on his hands chose to start making an annual record. However proclaimed, the fact is, summer 2007 in Britain was wet, with some places reporting 300 times their "normal" rainfall. For example in June the average rainfall across England was 140 millimetres (5.5 in), a figure more than double that experienced in a more normal year. Some unfortunate communities suffered more than one month's rain in just 24 hours. There were floods, deaths and great damage. The experts did what experts do best – they grabbed the opportunity for celebrity and smiled for the TV news cameras. Their analysis didn't make the weather any better but it did give many people justification for their fears of climate change.

But it all started so very differently. April was glorious with the air temperature as much as 5 degrees above normal expectation and rainfall well below average. On the 25$^{th}$ of April in Sussex they recorded a balmy temperature of 26.5 degrees. A Meteorological Office press release reported that spring 2007 was the warmest on record. This was more than enough to encourage the British media and TV pundits to hyperbolise on the summer we were all going to enjoy. Rent-a-quote "forecasters" told of the ducks flying north or early apple blossom that all portended another hot summer to rival that of 1976. While the Meteorological Office didn't allow themselves to endorse the wilder claims, their official long-term predictions did nothing other than suggest summer would be a great summer. As I prepared my clothes for my cruise, I stuffed several pairs of shorts into my bag.

But then came May. The famed high altitude jet stream moved south from its normal position north of the UK to track eastwards just below the English Channel. Just why the jet stream moved is a matter for others to speculate on. Perhaps it was Zeus playing with us mere mortals or George W Bush and his compatriots had been letting out too much carbon, but for whatever reason, we innocents knew nothing of all this. For us it just seemed May was a temporary "blip". But high above us the now stationary jet stream held the Azores high pressures at bay, well south of Britain. More perversely, the misplaced jet stream pulled low pressure after low pressure, down from the cold artic regions, to stagger across our green and pleasant land. While horrible floods plagued many inland cities and towns, on the coasts the swirling skies loured above sailors and we just got wetter and wetter. Never before had the metrological term "depression" seemed so apt. It rained and rained, and not surprisingly on the 15th July – in British folklore the fabled St Swithin's day, when if rain falls, another 40 rainy days follow – it rained. It would be late in August before the jet stream, inexplicably, returned north to its more usual location.

Apart from the obvious discomfort, the problem for sailors from the jet stream "malfunction" was not strong winds or summer gales. In fact, during my 94 days of the cruise, I was only port bound due to gales three times – once in Burnham-on-Crouch, then at Hartlepool and the third time at Ramsgate. The wind strengths I encountered, apart from than these three occasions, were fairly benign and quite within the bands a well designed yacht, such as Hobo, could easily manage. The real problem of this "summer of discontent" was the very unsettled nature of the weather and the resultant very confused forecasting. During what I had previously considered to be normal summer, a sailor could endure a brief Low pressure system knowing that a High pressure would soon build bringing a period of settled weather. While, of course, at some point another low would bear down, the High/Low pressure cycle would repeat and Highs would predominate.

Weather forecasters love high pressures as they allow confident prediction, boosting their egos and reputation. High pressures make weather forecasting easy, but the non-summer of 2007 was different and low pressures were like London buses – all coming at once. Pressure charts looked like the crazed scrawls of a delinquent child. Low pressure systems jostled with each other apparently removing any hope of accurate weather predictions.

The dubious nature of gangs of low pressure systems threatened the peace of mind of forecasters and sailors alike, but this was not the end of the problem. Once upon a time sailors only had the 6 hourly radio broadcast of the shipping forecast, today, in this very "electronic age", a coastal sailor has access to a myriad of weather forecasts from Gridded Binary (GRIB) files downloaded to computers, internet sites, digital TV stations and, of course, FM radio. On top of all this there is the ever helpful coast guard on the VHF radio repeating the Met Office shipping forecasts. However, this was one season when multiple choice merely multiplied the confusion. If one forecaster felt the need to include so much "variable" jargon to cover all weather possibilities then having access to five forecasts just multiplied the options. For a solo sailor trying to keep to the maxim of being a safe sailor, the daily diet of wildly changing forecasts, from numerable sources, proved to be pretty indigestible. In the summer of 2007 weather "windows" would appear in the forecasts, quickly close and then prove to be largely phantom. And of course the opposite was even more frustrating, many days were spent unnecessarily in port due to apparently "threatening" forecasts when the actual wind and seas remained benign.

I was to learn that the Met Office, owned by the tax payer and responsible for the majority of British weather forecasts, at this time didn't bother to check its forecasts with subsequent actual weather observations. In my opinion, it is crazy that it seems there is no independently published data on the accuracy of Met Office forecasts. In the epoch of school performance tables, hospital death rates, train arrival times *et cetera* this public funded body, responsible for predicting our island's weather smugly claims to be efficient, while refusing to publish any data that might confirm its success or reveal its failure.

My comment on the non-summer of 2007 has been written from the warmth of my Wapping lounge, yet the memory of weather we all experienced that year still holds the potential to cause me an inner shudder.

*On an adventure sometimes you find an undiscovered country or precious place, until then missing from your life, but mostly with adventure you just find yourself.*

# PART TWO

## GREENWICH TO GREENWICH
## AROUND THE BRITISH ISLES

*8 May – Day 1. Limehouse to Erith. Passage 14 nm, 3:15 hours*

So it began, my first steps on this adventure made in my 53rd year. Here at Limehouse basin, on the river Thames, I was very close to the now lost Ratcliffe Cross monument, or perhaps more correctly, the hamlet of Redcliffe, an ancient waterfront community where the records show, from as early as the year 1370, shipping moored while preparing for a voyage. Redcliffe and nearby Wapping were the starting points for Elizabethan adventurers such as Sir Hugh Willoughby and Sir Martin Frobisher while Captain James Cook later found both wife and home here. This immense maritime heritage is something that, perhaps, few of those now using the river probably ever reflect upon.

While today the Limehouse waterfront is an unromantic collection of modern apartment blocks, it was long dead, brave adventurers and the far off sea that filled my mind, as at 5pm, my crew, Phil Lloyd and I moved Hobo into the river lock, a literal heavy door opening out on to the mighty though grubby Thames. For me, at least, Limehouse lock gate appeared a symbolic portal to another world, or maybe today, just an unlit exit from the urban zoo. Out we shot onto the confused greyish water, dreaming and hoping to find clearer, more settled streams to come. As skipper, I was immediately confronted by a mass of information battling for primacy. Where is that boat full of tourists going? Can I avoid the fast Clipper catamaran full of commuters? And what about the bully-boy tugs with their train of lighters full of the London's waste off to another landfill? The river, at the poignantly named Cuckold Point, opposite the glass towers on Canary Wharf, is a busy chaotic thoroughfare and hardly welcoming. But I was there and sailing my choice.

Inevitably, despite a delayed departure and a few days of pseudo planning, it had still been a rush. It appeared as if I was only half ready and there were many small problems still to be resolved. But it's hard to believe the departure of any ship was achieved without problems. I felt a need to begin the voyage rather than spend more days marina bound and mentally "stressed out" with detail. I had chosen to meet and deal with the "snags" as I sailed the first few days of the cruise. After all, I was not leaping off onto the unknown wide ocean – famous words and, hopefully, not my last.

From Limehouse we motor sailed down river with the ebb tide and past the site of the old Deptford Royal Dockyard, the place where Goriana herself, Queen Elizabeth I, in April 1581, knighted a kneeling sailor named Francis Drake on his return from circumnavigating the globe. Looking at the now abandoned wharves and grey council housing, it is hard to believe that once the riverside was overhung with bow sprits, masts and anchors and the smell of tar and oakum permeated the taverns and warehouses. Then came the symbolic starting point of my voyage, Greenwich and its zero degrees Prime Meridian line, a glorious building and park which the departing sailors of past centuries would still recognise, on and out to the new, represented by the Millennium Dome and the Thames Barrier. Then Barking creek with its own grim barrier and its sewer outfall – so different today from the year 1722 when Daniel Defoe wrote of Barking's healthy fleet of fishing smacks plying the river to help feed the stomachs of Londoners. The river Thames, over the last 50 years, has lost so much life and colour with today's sailing yacht looking somehow alien, but alien or not we sailed on and down stream to pick up a borrowed mooring off Erith Yacht Club. Just 14 nautical miles and a mere 3¼ hours, but as the light rapidly faded, we chose to stop and settled down to what would be a surprisingly bumpy night. The river's ebb tide flows quickly around this south bend of the river, but the lack of moorings on the more sheltered north bank, combined with the filthy smell of the Rainham Marshes landfill site, meant we had little other choice. While relaxing before dinner I added notes to my "jobs to do". During the afternoon, with the freshening westerly wind, we had sailed using just the number three jib and I noticed that the forestay seemed slack and the boat domestic battery weak. I also realised I needed to re-read the user guide to the newly fitted VHF marine radio.

The passage down the Thames from London was necessary, but hardly fun. This historic waterway is now largely a post-industrial wasteland. Whereas once it perhaps offered stopping off points, the river bank today has nowhere a boat can safely spend the night or await a favourable tide. Unfortunately, the Port of London Authority seem to regard small craft with a type of contempt, and between St Katherine's Dock and Gravesend, a distance of 30 nautical miles, there are no riverside public jetties, pontoons or public mooring buoys. My passage plan took account of this marine depravation and hence the overnight stop at Erith Yacht Club. Early next morning, I intended using the whole ebb tide to exit the Thames and reach a turning point off Southend-on-Sea, where we would then butt the next foul tide and sail north along the Essex coast to Burnham-on-Crouch.

This first night I commenced what would become my bed-time routine by sliding into a body shaped old sleeping bag – perhaps looking like an Egyptian mummy but without all the unpleasant organ removal. The sleeping bag has an interesting story – and yes I accept the term interesting is relative to one's state of mind. The sleeping bag is 38 years old – yes I'm sure, although I agree it's hard to believe. I bought it from a camping store in Teignmouth, Devon when I was a mere 15 years old. At the time there was to be an overnight pop music festival at Newton Abbot racecourse, and myself and a friend – I can't remember exactly whom – thought we'd share in the then fashionable Woodstock vibe. Disappointingly, of course, none of the music acts were "stars" and free love was noticeably absent. I recall using the bag that night and somehow it has remained with me over the years and probably 20 or so different home addresses. So, on the first night of my new adventure, enveloped inside this ancient "winding sheet", I then pulled a new duvet over the top. Just after midnight I awoke almost cooked. So out of the bag and back under the duvet. This had to become comfortable at some point, although I did, over the coming weeks, try every bunk on Hobo.

*9 May – Day 2. Erith to Burnham-on-Crouch. Passage 54 nm, 13:30 hours*

I always think its important to establish routine when away from home but listening to the 5.20am shipping forecast is not one of my favourite rituals. This day the forecast suggested light winds with a strongwesterly arriving "later". If we truly had 12 hours before the south westerly gale, then we had a "weather window" to reach Burnham-on-Crouch, approximately 50 nautical miles to the east. Neither the town of Erith nor Gravesend appeared to offer us a favourable place to await better weather so, after a brief "conference" over a mug of breakfast tea, Phil and I decided to accept the less than ideal prospect of perhaps motor sailing for a significant portion of our passage. If the gale arrived earlier than forecast, we still had the possibility of diverting south to the safety of the Medway Estuary. However, at sea, seldom are things quite that simple. The entrance of the Medway at Sheerness has a tidal gate for small sailing yachts in that entry is only really possible at slack water or on the ingoing flood. If Hobo were to "bolt" for the safety of the Medway, our entry couldn't be achieved until the afternoon.

From Erith out to the sea one passes under the QE II bridge and past Tilbury docks and the quays of gloomily named Gravesend. The lower river Thames at this point east is grubby, lacking any of the niceties found west of London on the upper reaches above Chelsea. Soon the shoreline was all oil refineries and power stations. The long dead generations of valiant sailors, who had used the Thames to reach London, wouldn't recognise this ancient waterway. So it was with little regret I left my home river and headed out into the greater Thames estuary. The green channel buoy mysteriously named Ovens, on Gravesend Reach, marked the furthest point I had previously sailed. Prior to this day I had never sailed anywhere east or north of this point on the river. Consequently every port from Gravesend and north to Inverness and from there south to Plymouth was to be a new experience. Every harbour entry and every exit was to be a first time event. All my previous sailing experience in Britain was on the south coast between Plymouth and Brighton. So, as the greater estuary opened before me, it all appeared 'a brave new world'.

Unfortunately, along with the new horizon came an old problem. An engine fault that had, a week before, shown itself outside Limehouse marina recurred with greater effect. Off Southend-on-Sea, while benefiting from the last of the ebb tide, the engine revolutions began to fluctuate and fall. The boat speed dropped from 6 knots to 3.2 knots and then to 2.7. Knowing we were only about half way to Burnham, this was worrying, but the brightening sky and still favourable tide led us to conclude that, as the wind freshened from the west, if worst came to the worst, we could sail before the breeze and still arrive at our destination. So, with the variable light breeze, we continued and, in time, headed northeast to seaward of the Maplin sands. Soon a new problem materialised when all the yacht's electrical instruments suddenly failed. A quick check below suggested to me the main switch panel, complete with circuit breakers, was without power. After struggling to check the domestic battery – we carried two batteries, one for starting the engine and one for all the domestic electrical systems – buried far aft under the cockpit and cramped double berth, I realised the problem must be between the battery and switch panel. More investigation work revealed that there was a single primary fuse fitted before the breakers. This badly fitted item had slipped from its holder thereby causing all navigational instruments to fail. Clearly, this was something I needed to improve when, and if, we reached Burnham.

Burnham, while a fabled yachting town, is difficult to reach from all points lying to the south. First Maplin sands merge into Foulness sands, and a long sandbank spit serves as a further obstacle to craft. Approaching Burnham-on-Crouch from the Thames, sailors on passage are able to see the entrance, but they still have to sail on a further 8 nautical miles northeast to round Whitaker beacon, before doubling back the 8 nautical miles to the southwest. Naturally, the normal tidal activity of the river adds to the challenge. During my passage planning I had failed to recognise just how much this would increase the time needed to reach Burnham. By 15:37 Hobo was bowling along before a freshening southwesterly wind and nearing Whitaker beacon. Of course, wind that was fun to sail before was a challenge to beat against. On rounding the sand spit, we then spent the next three hours beating up the narrow channel against both wind and tide. As the strong winds for "later" mentioned in the early morning shipping forecast arrived, we battled up the Crouch, facing rain squalls and rapidly failing light. It was a hard three hours and the town of Burnham was to welcome our arrival with their combined yacht club's racing fleet charging at us through the mass of mooring buoys. What, to them, was an exhilarating couple of hours evening racing, for us, represented one last challenge after an eventful day. However, we still had one last drama to deal with. After battling the spring ebb and dodging the racing fleet, the problem engine again began to lose power. I was forced to ferry glide Hobo toward the entrance to Burnham yacht harbour, while wondering how quickly we might launch the anchor, if the engine failed before we got safely out of the tide. Luckily, and with a certain amount of skill, I glided Hobo through the entrance and straight into the first available pontoon berth. Once the boat was tidied, with sails flaked and under cover, I said a silent and private prayer of thanksgiving. The wind howled and the rain beat down hard. The ugly thought of not having achieved Burnham and having being blown back out into the north sea, with its sand banks, to spend a night facing the gale, was not something likely to help me sleep.

It had taken 13½ hours to complete the 54 nautical miles from Erith. During this passage I learned that I needed to spend more time on passage planning; the engine problem meant we could not safely enter a river against wind and tide; there were several aspects of the boat I needed to improve. None of this would surprise an experienced sailor, but, for me, I was still very much learning about cruising.

But then to be fair, this was only day two.

*10 – 14 May. Days 3 – 7*

The bad weather had then truly settled over Burnham-on-Crouch and as sailing would not be possible for several days Phil, my crew of 48 hours left the boat and returned home. This combined with the realisation that the engine problem had yet to be solved dictated that I would have a "jobs" day. Being in a town proudly dedicated to the sport of yachting, and having three well stocked chandleries within walking distance of the marina, was no hardship. I set about tackling the long list of faults so far discovered on the 70 nautical mile trip from Limehouse. In addition to the normal jobs, such as tightening shackles and re-rigging the safety line, I set out to try and cure the engine and electrical problems.

After checking the battery voltage and using a mains charger, I realised that Hobo's battery wasn't holding its electrical charge. So a new 70 amp hour marine grade battery was bought and fitted. To ensure the problem of the slipped fuse didn't recur, I rewired the power supply directly to the bank of circuit breakers. The engine problem was much more difficult. Several phone calls to various Volvo agents didn't offer much encouragement. However, a friend with a selection of clear plastic fuel lines helped identify the existence of the troublesome diesel "bug" – a living organism that sometimes lives happily in a dark diesel tank.

To me, the idea of a living micro organism or "bug" that can thrive in diesel fuel, contained inside a stainless steel tank, was quite a surprise. And for those of you who don't know, here are the facts. Sometime ago, due to pressure largely from urban dwelling "green" lobby groups, manufacturers of petrodiesel started to add 5% of new biodiesel, brewed from vegetable oil, to the traditional, very ancient, straight from the earth variety. This biodiesel, in the small quantities currently added to traditional petrodiesel, burns happily in cars, trucks and marine engines and powers yachts without anyone noticing any change. But – and here's the rub – the bio part of the diesel, being young, is still "alive", and when left for several months in a dark, damp place, and yes, on a boat there is condensation, even inside the fuel tank, the bio bugs multiply and set up thick, black, gooey colonies. These black, gooey townships, shaken, rather than stirred, by the motion of the yacht, can then be sucked from the fuel tank by the means of the fuel pump. Fuel lines, filters and even engine injectors can all suffer thrombosis – the engine loses power and the yacht loses forward propulsion and vital steerage. Of course, for any car driver, having an engine failure while on the road, is merely inconvenient, but for a sailor, having a engine failure while at sea, the situation can be categorised as "distress". This fuel problem for yachtsmen is serious and can result in life threatening situations. But at present, while many yacht owners and marine engineers know of the biodiesel threat to our "life and liberty", governments and regulators ignore the problems of seafarers.

The recommended means of eliminating this very troublesome alien life form is the horrible and difficult task of cleaning out the fuel tank. Unfortunately, as with the battery location, the Hanse 301 yacht designer had chosen to site the fuel tank under the double berth fitted in the narrow space beneath the cockpit sole. Worse still, the builder had installed it in a manner as to make the tank inspection hatch totally inaccessible. While not a perfect solution, a trip to the chandler produced an electric oil change pump. Using this pump I sucked out 15 litres of diesel from the tank and then added a large dose of Marine 16, the anti-bug fuel treatment recommended by magazine

Practical Boat Owner. After refuelling and a long engine test with Hobo steaming up and down the Crouch river I believed I had cured the engine problem.

When the morning wake-up call is a violent flapping of halyards and sail cover, you quickly realise home is far away and you are on a boat. Five a.m. doesn't seem like a good hour when the sky is a grubby blanket, and the drone of the wind tells a story of forces far from the remembered comfort of the bedroom. After only four days I was yet to adjust to my new environment. My fingers were already raw and felt like they were frostbitten. I've not experienced the curse of Captain Scott or Alpine climbers, but I'm sure the ache from bleeding finger tips must be similar. The hardware of a sailing yacht combined with the cold May weather had punished my soft, computer keyboard ready, fingers.

But another jobs day demanded my attention, and I felt obliged to check on deck to confirm the annoying flapping and banging was merely an equipment tantrum, rather than something more terminal. Then tea. Tea is a must on a boat and I feel unable to trust anyone who doesn't like tea. When the day feels more like a prison sentence than a boon, tea is the rescuer. Frustratingly for me, the low air temperatures experienced up to the point of the "ides of May" had been enough to upset the "don't gas me" automatic cut off device on the boat cooker and it always took several attempts before a sustainable flame was achieved. I think early cave men had similar trouble. But persistence pays in the end and a steaming mug of tea in hand helped cheer the senses. But, of course, steam on a boat is not a good thing. Apart from the windows, it turns reading glasses into a "shower screen". But the price is worth paying for this simple, hot fluid, a foreign import brought to these islands by hardy seamen four centuries ago. A period when today's hardship of being boat bound on the river Crouch would have seemed like paradise. Unlike the Tudor and Elizabethan sailor, I had the wonder of modern fleece clothing, a layer of softness and the illusion of real warmth. Today a mariner's lot is all electronics, frustration and micro pile fibre.

I had, by then, discovered I lacked the discipline of writer Anthony Trollope, who, in the nineteenth-century, wrote for two hours each morning before breakfast and before his paid employment at the Post Office. If I could have been like him I would have already written a description of the people and streets of Burnham. But exhaustion, or perhaps more frequently, stretched emotions and bruised fingers, meant that, despite having things to record, I couldn't always face the frightening blank page and the challenge of linking characters in black ink.

I had also the realisation that, sailing apart, I was on a tour of British seaside towns. This was to be an adventure spent in the places that have largely been forsaken by the British public. Whereas, prior to the 1970s, people flocked to the coasts to enjoy their annual holiday, the arrival of foreign package tours and thereafter budget flights, resulted in the demise of the "traditional" English seaside family holiday. Walking the streets of Burnham rekindled long forgotten memories of my childhood when cloudy skies, bracing air and the smell of fish and chips combined to offer an escape from the industrial sprawl of England's midland. My Sunday spent in Burnham included a bacon sandwich and mug of tea in the Cabin Dairy Tea Rooms. Here was a no-nonsense breakfast with not a celebrity chef in sight. No one here asked me to specify the bread variety or if I wanted butter or margarine. Here the table cloth was reassuringly white plastic and I felt I had returned to a childhood holiday "home". Unfortunately this "home" was closed on Monday – a symptom of the silly disease of the English seaside, namely a sign declaring "out of season – weekends only".

However, encouraged by these childhood memories, for the boat I bought a brown "china" tea pot at the local Coop. You don't find many of either convenience in London.

*15 May – Day 8. Burnham to Harwich. Passage 40 nm, 7 hours*

I had been harbour bound for five days and, despite using the time to good effect to complete a number of jobs, I was impatient to move on. The May weather had improved from the early gale conditions, but still the forecast was hardly encouraging to a person who was now a solo sailor. I could see rain squalls, like so many hooded yobs at a bus station, charging from the southwest across the river Crouch. The dark grey shapes in the sky to windward seemed to reach down to the ground, blocking from sight, the features of land and sea that are so reassuring yet apparently temporal. Mentally I had committed myself to the passage and I prepared to get wet. A sailor must accept the squalls and pangs of discomfort. So at 11am I actioned my passage plan and departed from my secure pontoon and the civilised world of toilets, showers and terra firma. Within minutes the sky loured down upon me, the wind increased and rain fell. A mini tempest was hardly the start I wanted on this first leg of solo sailing. Hobo heeled before the gusts and accelerated, pushed down river by the southwesterly breeze. With two reefs needed to reduce the size of the mainsail and number three jib the autohelm device did the easy job. If only we could have swapped roles, with me on the tiller and the gismo hauling up the sails. But, on this thirty foot boat, I was the only manpower. Good technique would have to replace brute strength. A quartering sea and, what I estimated as 25 knots of wind – Hobo didn't have an anemometer – made for a lively sail for a fin keel, light displacement yacht such as a Hanse 301.

While the squalls, spring ebb and quartering sea created excitement, it was the offshore sand banks that provided the stuff of anxiety. My passage planning had shown the shoals but it was only when I approached the breaking waves that the significance of these natural hurdles started to become manifest. What had looked easy in the quiet of the cabin now screamed "death trap". Unfortunately, prior to leaving Burnham, none of the three yacht chandlers had been able to sell me the necessary navigational chart. Without this C1 Imray chart, I had planned my passage to Harwich using only the electronic Garmin 450 chart plotter and a composite chart showing just the Harwich harbour entrance. These limited resources perhaps led me to my unwise decision to cross the Gunfleet sandbank on the falling tide. However, as I approached this crossing point at 7.2 knots over the ground, the steep breaking white waves of shallow water ahead gave signs that perhaps this was not a sensible option. I soon realised good charts would be vital, as getting lost while driving around town is frustrating, to get lost at sea might mean a drowning.

In retrospect, and for those who may follow, I would advise any north bound yacht leaving the river Crouch to use the Swin channel to Wallet Spitway and close with the Clacton-on-Sea coast.

But to my small credit, I did belatedly recognise that crossing the Gunfleet would be reckless – or rather wreck likely – so I altered Hobo's course to the northeast. Yet my new route created another problem. With the sea conditions, the autohelm was unable to maintain a stable course and, yet, I needed to study the chart and, if possible, re-programme the route in the chart plotter. Even after dropping the mainsail and continuing under just the jib, leaving the helm unattended for more than a few moments created disorder rather than calm.

But with the wind and tide driving Hobo quickly onward an alternative course to Harwich was chosen. This entailed a gybe to north west of Gunfleet Beacon and sailing via the less than attractively named Medusa buoy toward Stone banks, and from there, into Harwich. This revised course would add considerably to the distance but, happily, I still had many hours of daylight. Sadly, my grasp of how to reprogram the very new chart plotter proved to be less than adequate. From this point forward navigational dead reckoning would have to serve me – I've never appreciated the term "dead" when applied to navigation – but testing conditions and situations are all very much part of adventure. And it was an adventure skirting the sandbanks, avoiding the cursed crab pots and gradually closing on the entrance to Harwich. The feeling of relief and childish satisfaction at making landfall after a challenging passage is part of sailor lore. This was to live the life of sailors down the centuries long before our centrally heated, carpeted and internet world removed the term survival from common understanding.

Harwich Harbour, doubtless no picture postcard view, that day to me looked truly wonderful. In this I mean it looked like a haven and somewhere to rest. However, before all the trials of the day were ended, there was still the requirement to find and pass through the sea lock at Shotley Point Marina. Fatigue must, at this point, have started to work upon my senses, because, as Hobo approached the recommended turning point to cross the deep water channel, I noticed – I could hardly miss them – two huge bright red light ships. A rapid inspection of the chart and chart plotter failed to reveal any note of the light ships or give any indication of the serious hazards they were so obviously guarding. As far as the charts were concerned there were no light ships, yet I could clearly see them. Of course, on any normal day I would have quickly realised, as Harwich is the home of Trinity House, the organisation responsible for maintaining lights and buoys, redundant light ships at anchor might be expected. Later, at just after 6pm, secure for the night in a sheltered marina berth at Shotley, oh how I laughed at my stupidity. And so ended my third day of sailing.

It had been another day of learning by experience. I learned, to my cost, that I could not rely on local yacht chandlers to supply charts for the next piece of adjacent coast. Also, passage planning without a bird's eye view of the hazards is less than satisfactory. While modern chart plotters are a fabulous boon for solo sailors, the small section of any chart viewable on the screen makes adequate comprehension of the greater area quite difficult. Using the chart plotter, electronically panning out, to gain sight of the complete route between two distant points, loses the type of detail vital to safe passage planning. I also learned when sailing solo it is fairly vital to have fully mastered the use and programming of any newly acquired electronic equipment.

*16 May – Day 9*

Harwich became my town for a day of rest and relaxation, a town where, for centuries, sailors have recharged themselves in taverns and tabernacles while, at the same time, inexplicably yearning to return to a watery world. However, today, just across the harbour, is the modern soulless equivalent, Felixstowe, now the UK's largest container port with its dockside piled high with multicoloured steel boxes like so much Lego.

Harwich is a pleasant town but suffering from neglect and lack of civic pride. Unfortunately, the local community, like so many others in England, has allowed town planners and corporate store parasites to vandalise the once neat streets. On the quayside where the small ferry from Shotley Marina arrives, the ornate Victoria Hotel is a monument to the type of self-respect the townsfolk once had. Unfortunately, only yards away from this wonderful building, is an example of the stark, concrete, brutalist architecture that has helped destroy a public sense of community and good taste. The horrid Trinity House building insults the eye like a yellow post-it note stuck on a Gainsborough painting. The minds that approved of this building were the same perhaps as those who approved the closing the quayside railway station that had once brought the public to the seaside and to board the packet ships that gave life to the harbour.

A walk up Harwich high street and along to Dovercourt reveals urban decay. So many vacant shop fronts – closed for business, boarded and symbols of failure. Glass fronted coffins on the main street where once there was commercial vibrancy and employment. Back in old Harwich there were once 26 taverns catering to the needs of sailors and the merchants who relied upon the harbour for their livelihood. Today the narrow streets create a feeling of Dickens' Miss Havisham's wedding breakfast – the people are absent but the table is still set and awaiting their return.

On the harbour-side there is yet another plaque "boasting" a connection to that ship the Mayflower. The captain was a Harwich man and Harwich now wishes to claim their share in the credit for creation of the American Nation. This apparent civic need to proclaim a Mayflower connection is very common. Any traveller who walks the harbour streets of southern England will notice how often town leaders choose to celebrate the Mayflower. This ship appears to have leap frogged all along the coast of England until it finally broke away from the land and headed out into the Atlantic. That the Mayflower passengers so hated

England and their fellow countrymen they chose to leave it and endure the horrors a voyage to the new world entailed, suggests to me there must be other ships better deserving of commemoration. The seas of the world were once traversed by vessels from these shores, and the vigour and spirit of these patriotic crews, who loved their country and helped make it rich, deserve to be recognised, rather than one small ship of religious malcontents.

*17 May – Day 10. Harwich to Lowestoft. Passage 43 nm, 7:30 hours*

The day's sail to Lowestoft, Suffolk was to be another solo adventure and again the weather was hardly encouraging. The drizzle and poor visibility made my departure less than glorious. No waving crowds or loved ones on the jetty. Just the cold and angular red and green buoys that mark the route away from shelter and lead to the North Sea. I left at 10:46 to take the full ebb tide, using the current to speed Hobo northwards, following the coast line. The light easterly breeze gradually increased and the visibility improved until, by lunchtime, there was some welcome sunshine. However, it was me alone on the sea. What I started to notice about sailing on the east coast, so different from on the south, is the almost total lack of other leisure craft. Hour after hour on passage and hardly another vessel ever comes into sight.

Compared to the previous two passages, the route from Harwich to Lowestoft offered few, if any problems. Once away from the big ship channel, I used the Sledway to sail for Orfordness. The only notable point of the passage was the white dome of Sizewell nuclear power station. This was memorable, but I much preferred the sight of the town of Lowestoft, and after the required VHF radio call to the harbour control to seek permission to enter, Hobo slipped into the old fishing dock, now home to a marina professional managed by the Royal Norfolk and Suffolk Yacht Club.

*18 May – Day 11*

This was my eleventh day aboard Hobo. Eleven days in the cramped space a sailing yacht provides and living the intense 24 hour existence that is a sailor's life. The other world, the one detached from the direct concerns of boat, weather and passage, seemed very far away. This is definitely a bizarre form of escapism where normal triviality is replaced with profoundly involved matters of wellbeing. I found myself fully immersed in a "life" that was without commuting, offices, TV, daily post et cetera. Life hadn't slowed, it had just become more intimate. Things external were in a world only as far as I could reach. The world of the live-a-board is all felt. It is not abstract but very physical. The world I inhabited warmed or cooled me; wet me and, sometimes, fed me. The solitude that comes with this new world is contemplative and intense. As a first time solo sailor, I realised that perhaps real depth of thought and learned experience is only achieved when, like a monk or mystic, solitude is fully embraced.

After ten days living on a boat, it was interesting to realise how one comes to value the civility of a simple chair or the utility of the shower block. What we take for granted at home becomes cherished luxury when one lives on a boat. A sailor soon learns to value simple pleasures. Also, I had been really enjoying rediscovering the pleasure of radio. From my early childhood days, life had been enriched by the sound of the pirate radio stations and night-time radio Luxembourg. Radio has offered me far more than it ever cost. This is surely democratic entertainment for the masses. No need of satellite subscription or internet connection or the Hollywood movie brain washers. Radio – this is the stuff of imagination and innocent pleasure.

Lowestoft, with its beach promenade and wonderful yacht club, is a "must visit" port on a cruise around Britain. Not just for the welcoming and comfortable clubhouse – with their wonderful Victorian toilets – but because Lowestoft is the last all weather, all tide harbour south of the Humber, over 100 nautical miles to the north. Strangely, although I was later to find this all too common, despite the town being on the sea and having a large harbour, Lowestoft didn't have a yacht chandler. This seaside town has the usual corporate shopping stores but nowhere for a sailor to obtain spares and items necessary to maintain a vessel. But a 45 minute walk to the beautiful freshwater Oulton Broad brought me to Jeckells & Son where helpful staff were able to meet the needs that businessmen of Lowestoft should have been able to supply.

Lowestoft is the point in the cruise around Britain marking one end of the sole unavoidable overnight passage. Unless you are sailing a yacht that can safely take to the ground at low water, the north Norfolk coast and the Wash area offers no convenient haven to break the journey to or from the Humber. Both the almanac and Pilot books detail the harbour options but none looked inviting to a yacht that had 1.7 metres of very pointed fin keel. So this reality determined, that if I wanted to avoid a solo passage of approximately 24 hours, for the next leg of the cruise I would need to find willing crew. Happily for me, Terry Naude and Jim Guckian, two friends from Greenwich Yacht Club volunteered to help, and, after many cabin conferences, we planned our passage north to Grimsby.

*19 May – Day 12. Lowestoft to Grimsby. Passage 102 nm, 21:09 hours*

Careful study of the tidal atlas revealed complications to

the "normal" simplistic idea of six hour ebb and a six flood. The huge watery expanses of The Wash and the Humber estuary, filling and emptying every twelve hours results in what appears to be a notional tidal roundabout or pivot point somewhere off The Wash. My conclusion was that any passage plan tracking north from Lowestoft should allow the mariner to use the northward current while navigating the narrow channel between the Norfolk coast and the offshore sand banks; then, avoid the southwesterly stream into the Wash but catch the northward flow into the Humber. The written explanation here is confusing and to be honest it isn't much easier on the water. The fact that, on the day we chose to start our passage, the tidal range between low and high water at Lowestoft was just 2 metres whereas the range 100 nautical miles away at our destination on the Humber was 6.4 metres, confirms the need to study the tidal flows very carefully.

On a passage lasting between 18 and 24 hours we wanted to utilise two full tides going north and only have to butt one foul tide coming south. Furthermore, the Saturday departure from Lowestoft and our passage north had to allow for arrival at Grimsby on Sunday with an ingoing tide. While the dock gates at Grimsby were on free-flow access from high water plus or minus two hours, the ebb on the Humber can achieve a speed of 4.5 knots and this would make entry impossible for a yacht such as Hobo with a small diesel. So lots of paper and pencil was used to estimate the best departure time and arrival options based on the assumption of an average passage speed of 5 knots.

It was at noon on a bright, sunny, but cold, Saturday we set off for Grimsby. The Met Office forecast suggested a south-westerly breeze of force 4 to 5 dropping later to variable 2 to 3. Having a full crew for the passage was very reassuring but for me still a novelty. After asking for and receiving permission to exit the harbour, we quickly raised sails and bounded forward on a broad reach as the fresh south-westerly breeze kicked against the opposing tide for the last hour of the south bound current.

As the maxim suggests, "all roads lead north" and this is very true off the Norfolk coast. The chart indicates there's first Corton Roads then Gorleston leading on to Yarmouth and Caister; four "roads" marking the coastal passage inside the Holm and Scoby offshore sand banks. The chart symbols suggested there were 30 or so wind turbines planted on these banks and their 68 metre height makes them a useful warning as to the location of the shoals. These strangely named "wind farms" – can they really cultivate wind? – are being built in our coastal waters and, whatever their questionable value in the environmental battle to reduce carbon emissions, they represent a real safety hazard to small craft that in fine weather and the right state of tide might hitherto have chosen to sail cross the sands.

When considering offshore wind turbines, those of you who, like me and all other sailors, love the natural environment, need to employ rational thought rather than choose to merely mouth fuzzy slogans about green energy. It is fact and perhaps the inconvenient truth that if offshore wind power were really a financially viable energy source, the world's seas would still be crisscrossed by fleets of Tea Clippers and towering four masted sailing Barques. These wind powered ships would still be serving the cause of world trade and feeding our appetite for consumer goods. But of course, sadly, commercial wind powered ships are no more. Over one hundred years ago all merchant sailors and corporate investors recognised that wind power was unreliable and unpredictable. Masters of wind powered ships could not guarantee how long any journey would take or, if indeed, a ship would get there at all. This is the truth about wind as a commercially viable energy source. However, it appears politicians of the UK government are not sailors, nor do they have any real understanding of history or economics. Surely, if there was wisdom in Westminster, ministers would publicly acknowledge that the time of commercial wind power, like that of windmills and steam engines, has passed. Low carbon generation of electricity will be achieved through new technologies not old. Sadly for both the environment and we sailors, one day there might be as many as 7,000 of these giant turbine "monuments" stuck in the sea bed around the coast of our island. The very nature of our coast and seas will be changed forever. From my understanding, as a long time lover of all things natural, mass offshore wind turbines represent an attack on our marine environment by the seemingly hypocritical, metropolitan based, doom merchants who earn their salaries by exploiting our collective fears of Armageddon. I find it bizarre to consider that one day, port to port passage sailing – surely one of the most environmentally friendly means of family transport – around Britain might not be possible given 7,000 man made obstacles towering from the seabed across our once friendly coastal waters.

The wind direction and strength assured our fast progress along the coast, although, due to the gusts, we had to take in first one reef then a second. By 17:00 we were off Cromer and 32 nautical miles from Lowestoft. But, with the wind still increasing and quite squally, we had to reduce sail still further to a 3rd reef and then resort to dropping the main altogether. However, as the tide slackened and we headed away from the coast, the squalls passed, and under single reefed main and jib, we looked for the first sight of a red buoy marking the channel between Blakeney overfalls and shoals guarded by West Sheringham cardinal. This was our entry point to what represents a long corridor leading north between Docking shoal and the Race bank. As the tide turned and darkness fell, we settled down to what would feel like a long night. The wind eased, but, of course, this left an uncomfortable confused sea and Hobo without sufficient boat speed to reduce her rolling motion. More than one us felt the early signs of mal de mar. Our eyes were strained, searching the dark horizon for the flashing lights marking the various buoys. As this was the main shipping channel there was now an increase in traffic and we had to alter course three times during the night to avoid crossing ships or even more dangerous, those overtaking us from astern. At midnight the wind dropped still further and the foul tide dictated our decision to motor sail. At 02:48 we passed Inner Dowsing and watched the lights of towns along the Lincolnshire coast. At 04:00 we looked for the Protector buoy, but, despite the reassuring name, our slow progress started to increase my anxiety. The issue causing concern was the need to arrive at the Humber with a favourable tide. The nautical almanac warned of a 4.5 knot ebb current pouring out of the estuary and this we had to avoid. If we failed to arrive at Grimsby by 09:30 we would be forced to divert to Spurn Head and anchor to await an ingoing favourable tide. This would mean our passage time would be extended by at least 6 hours and my two crew would miss their train back to London and consequently, be late getting to work on Monday.

The end of the so-called "graveyard watch" coincided with the increasing effect of the night time cold and damp. No-one on board was in good humour but happily the dawn sun started to improve conditions. We were making progress, mile after mile slipping beneath the keel, and we could now make out, on the horizon, the wide entrance to the Humber and the rows of ships awaiting their scheduled time for pilots or berthing. After a little confusion over the depths available for our route over Haile Sand, we passed our namesake channel marker buoy – Hobo – and proceeded via the Bull channel towards Grimsby.

Entry to the Fish Dock at Grimsby is simple once the harbour's narrow gap has been identified amidst all the grey stone and concrete of the outer dock wall. It took some time to spot the gap – florescent spray paint marking the entrance would really have helped. But by 08:43 we were alongside Meridian quay within the very post-industrial setting of number 2 Fish Dock. The tiring passage of 21:09 hours was over and this marked what I expected to be the only overnight passage of the entire cruise around Britain. After a hasty clear up, the crew of Hobo and I headed into town and enjoyed a cooked breakfast at the nearby Asda – the best thing about Asda for the itinerant sailor is they are often open a full 24 hours and they have a café. When the last piece of bacon had been consumed, I said my farewells to Terry and Jim and they left me for the train and a fast return to London.

*21-23 May. Days 14 – 16*

I spent the next three days in Grimsby, a guest of the Humber Cruising Association (HCA) which manages the Meridian Marina. While the members of the HCA couldn't have been more friendly or helpful to a refugee from the sea, Grimsby, as a town, is a sad monument to many years of bad governance. Grimsby is, I was told, the largest fish market in the UK and probably Europe. The docks that were built to serve the vast fishing fleet extend over a huge area between the town and the Humber estuary. But now the vibrant fishing fleet is gone and with it the thousands of livelihoods for hardworking people. Fish still arrives at Grimsby and the market flourishes, but today it is not brave boats but huge refrigerated trucks that bring the catch.

The dock area which used to support so many jobs in the trawler and fishing service industry is now largely derelict. Where once wharves were home to hundreds of trawlers and alive with fishermen and tradesmen, now there's nothing but discarded plastic fish boxes and the remnants of lost commerce. The surrender of the UK fishing industry to the EU fleet has had another bad effect on Grimsby. The huge, bleak dock area is now an effective barrier between the town and the Humber estuary. The town seemingly has its back to a decaying abandoned fish dock rather than the vibrant and life affirming waterway. For a person visiting the town centre it is possible to miss the fact that Grimsby is beside the sea. Equally unfortunate, for those arriving by sea at the fish dock, it is possible to be unaware a Victorian city exists a short 30 minute walk to the west. This is crazy. The dock area owned and run by the Associated British Ports is now a people-free zone. Natives or visitors are not welcome and only the very determined are likely to walk the streets, where historic ice houses used to cascade huge blocks into the holds of the waiting trawlers. The surviving commercial ship dock has a bold red brick tower worthy of an Italian pope. This 300 foot tower was built in 1852 to hold 30,000 gallons of water, for use as hydraulic power for the lock gates and cranes, and it once proclaimed civic pride to those arriving or leaving Grimsby. Now the tower is imprisoned within the Associated British Ports "Guantanamo" where only the hard hats and truck drivers are allowed free entry.

Another example of the folly of the governance of Grimsby is that, despite being Europe's largest fish market, it is impossible to eat a fish meal in the dock area. You can smell fish in the air and you have to step over fish skeletons, doubtless abandoned by greedy seagulls, but humans cannot breakfast, lunch or dine on fish; no cafés or bistros or restaurants, no chairs, tables or tablecloths; no smiling waiters or smell of grilled seafood. Nothing. Imagine a French St Malo, or St Vaast or American San Francisco's Fisherman's wharf or even Brixham in Devon without any cafes or restaurants. Unthinkable yes, but this is Grimsby fish docks.

Yet the reason for a sailor to visit Grimsby is not the Victorian heritage or the fish docks it is the people of the Humber Cruising Association. These part-time sailors have managed to create a flourishing club in a small part of the waste land that is today's fish dock. As a members' cooperative they have organised the pontoons, the slipway yacht hoist, showers and a small, but welcoming clubhouse. It is the best of Lincolnshire behind a steel mesh fence and hidden from the majority population of Grimsby. The excellent value, daily berthing charge of just £11.75 for a 30 foot yacht, only helps confirm my opinion of Grimsby as worth a visit.

Have you heard the one about the three ex-miners and the ex-fireman? No, well, you might if you sample a pint of bitter in the clubhouse. You might also hear stories of the tough life at the coal face, working the drift or the belts. Yet this is not a scene from the wonderful movie *Brassed Off*, the people here at the HCA are very full of life. They share the fellowship created of men, who spent their working lives, making something human out of hours spent in the dark underground. Ultimately, and after providing the fuel for the enterprise of the British Empire, they were exploited both by the trade unions and the National Coal Board. But being an unreconstructed romantic, I probably have understood more than I was supposed to see.

During one of my walks around the fish docks I spotted a faded red painted sign on a brick building, Madame DuFour and her Poissonniere. With this sign, what I believed to be an advertisement, I allowed myself to imagine that a French woman of the 19th century had here succeeded in the male dominated world of fishing. The idea that this woman could build a successful business appealed to my sensibility. Unfortunately, this was just an illusion as later in the bar of the HCA, I was told that the red sign was a mere fake, painted by a TV production company, who had used the docks to film a drama set in France. Another romantic illusion shattered.

My four days in Grimsby were spent in hard work catching up on the annual maintenance programme all yachts require. Due to the short period between my taking a share of ownership of Hobo, and the start of the cruise, it had not been possible to clean off the hull and renew the antifouling. Boat speed achieved over the 258 nautical miles so far completed, suggested to me a dirty bottom and less than pristine propeller. Happily, the HCA, with Keith, then their excellent yard master, came to my rescue, and on the morning following my arrival, Hobo was gently lifted out of the water and placed into a cradle in the yard. Unfortunately, Grimsby, like Lowestoft and so many other towns, today does not have a chandler, so once again HCA was able to help out, supplying the vital antifouling. After I resolved a few problems removing the corroded folding propeller – a necessary precursor to replacing the anode on the sail drive – two coats of fresh antifouling were applied and Hobo once again was ready to continue the trip – hopefully now with a little more boat speed. The cost of the lift out, spray off, use of cradle and re-launch was significantly less than the costs quoted by south coast boat yards. I can thoroughly recommend a visit to HCA.

*24 May – Day 17. Grimsby to Filey Bay. Passage 54 nm, 9:06 hours*

While resting between jobs, I had pondered long and hard over the next bit of my cruise. I was sailing solo once more and after four days "out of the saddle" I needed to get back into a sailing routine. The next obvious destination on the east coast passage north is the town of Whitby, but unfortunately it is a 75 nautical mile distance from Grimsby. I preferred to find something less arduous. The almanac offered me the prospect of a drying harbour of Bridlington, fine for bilge keel yachts perhaps but not for Hobo. However, a little local knowledge gained from the sailors at HCA, provided me with another option. They told me of how Scarborough harbour had recently been dredged and pontoon berths were available to visitors. So I decided to try for Scarborough. However, as an alternative option, there were overnight anchorages possible close inshore to Flamborough Head and in Filey Bay.

Hobo was re-launched and I took the afternoon tide out of the Humber and turned once more northwards. The Met Office weather forecast was for southwesterly wind force 3-4 veering northwesterly later. At 12:30, in weak hazy sunshine, and with the ebb tide, I hoisted full sail and headed Hobo towards Spurn Head. With a speed over ground of 6.8 knots the turning point arrived quickly and I gybed bringing Hobo on to a northerly course and towards the headland of Flamborough 35 nautical miles distant.

However, 35 nautical miles, even with a speed over ground of 7 knots, takes 5 hours, and as I reached the headland, the tide started to turn against me. Despite hugging the shallows under the cliffs, progress slowed dramatically and I started to consider my options. Scarborough was still a very long way off. As the weather looked settled for the next 24 hours, I decided I would divert to Filey Bay and spend my first night at anchor.

At 21:36, close inshore, in 5 metres of water, I anchored off St Oswalds Church, Filey. It was then dark and following what felt like a tiring 54 nautical miles and over nine hour passage, I started to relax. Of course anchoring in a fin keel yacht is not as relaxing as being tied to a pontoon. There is always the question of how much anchor warp to let out and taking bearings to gauge any possible drift. I also set the anchor light and placed a yellow post-it note on the bulkhead above the chart table giving the compass bearing I'd need to use to exit the bay if the weather changed for the worse during the night.

While in the folklore of cruising sailors lying to anchor is considered to be a mark of the purist, lying to anchor for the solo sailor is not without discomfort. It is rare to find an anchorage where the turn of the tide doesn't create an annoying mini swell, enough to rock the boat and jostle every pot, bottle or pencil stowed within it. Additionally, for a fin keeler there is a tendency for the yacht to scud about, swinging to the far ends of the anchor warp and creating the illusion of drifting. And then, should the weather change and the wind turn onshore, there is the challenge of recovering the anchor. On a thirty foot boat without anchor windlass, electric or manual, the physical strength needed to recover the anchor and chain is considerable. Add to this the drag on the boat caused by wind and the action of waves and recovering an anchor for a solo sailor is a trial of strength. Sailing folklore is fine, but the reality of spending a night at anchor needs to be acknowledged.

Later on my cruise I was to discover something rotten had lain close to where I spent my night at anchor – the wreck of the pirate ship Bon Homme Richard. It is a bizarre story and one that involves the so-called "special relationship" between little Britain and big USA. Back in 1779 a Scotsman, commanding five borrowed French ships, harassed and stole from commercial shipping around the Ulster and Scottish coast. Sailing under a flag of the American Revolution, this Scotsman attacked two British Naval ships off Flamborough Head on the 23rd of September. While seemingly victorious in this sea battle, his French, re-flagged American ship, later sank, just off Filey. The pirate's name? Captain John Jones, now celebrated by the American nation as John Paul Jones, his body entombed in marble and bronze and treated to much ceremonial pomp, in the Naval Academy Chapel, at Annapolis, Maryland.

*25 May – Day 18. Filey to Scarborough. Passage 26 nm, 5:50 hours*

The town of Filey is a remnant of those days when the successful businessmen of Yorkshire chose to have weekends by the sea. For their use imposing terraces of Victorian houses were built facing the wonderful view, all neatly lined up by local builders, to be on the level and good for carriages or walking. On the beach below can be seen another bit of living history. Native fishing boats known as Cobles. The design of these boats evolved to allow for launching and recovery through the waves onto the beach. These wooden clinker built boats have survived the passage of centuries. The advent of Glass Reinforced Plastic and other newfangled concepts haven't made the wooden Cobles any less viable, and here these boats are not museum exhibits. Here Cobles are used by today's fishermen of Filey.

At the early time of 04:30 I viewed the dawn with little enthusiasm, but then solid grey skies are rarely encouraging whatever the time of day. However, I wanted to take the last 4 hours of favourable tide north to Whitby and a little discomfort is, of course, part of sailing. The 05:20 forecast was for southwesterly wind, but as I headed out the bay I was greeted by drizzle and a northerly. There was a short, wind against tide, choppy sea so I chose to motor sail. By 07:00 the wind had dropped leaving a confused sea and yet more rain, so I decided to divert to Scarborough. However, by 08:00 the wind returned, and this time from the west, so once more Whitby looked possible. Unfortunately, as the tide turned against me, so did the wind, and I was forced to beat against the current. This became a battle, me against the elements, and I looked for, and counted off the bays along the shore that marked progress towards Whitby. Alas, the progress was really painful, and at 10:00 I reluctantly accepted defeat. It was just too uncomfortable and I have always maintained beating against the tide is something a cruising sailor shouldn't do except in an emergency. So off Robin Hood's Bay I reluctantly turned Hobo about and we sailed downwind back towards Scarborough. The feeling of relief was instantaneous. The boat's motion eased. I at last warmed up and was able to grab something to eat. Unfortunately, the autohelm, struggling with the following sea, drew too much electricity, and tripped the circuit breakers; but that was something I could attend to later. At 11:20 I was alongside a brand new pontoon in a very sheltered and now very sunny Scarborough harbour.

Scarborough proved to be a pleasant surprise to this well travelled Englishman.  After having in the past marvelled at the wonders of Venice and Bruges, I now found Scarborough. Perhaps, due to my ignorance, the beauty was unexpected, but still appreciated. Scarborough from the sea is dramatic, a sort of Monte Carlo, but with a huge 12th century castle. There is a sheltered crescent bay with a yellow sand beach and some magnificent buildings that, once again, proclaim past times when the English were confident, prosperous and public spirited. Before the rise of the centralised modern state and a socialist intelligentsia, councils and local businessmen worked together to build beautiful, graceful towns, where, those with jobs, could be proud of their identity and proclaim themselves Yorkshire men and women. For me the contrast between Scarborough and Grimsby couldn't be greater. Scarborough still has a civic pride that impresses a perhaps cynical southerner; the friendly people, great beer and wonderful British food; the rare treat of perfectly prepared fried chips at lunchtime; or that northern delight originally made in Lancashire, freshly baked Eccles cakes – so different from the cold stodgy insult sold wrapped in plastic by the supermarkets; and lastly, after dinner, the wonderful regional delicacy of Yorkshire curd tart, a divine sort of cross between cheesecake and quiche. If any of this food had been developed in France, they would surely have patented the brand and boasted to gourmets around the world of their regional specialities. In addition to all this, for visiting sailors, the harbour authority last year dredged the drying harbour and installed pontoons. So now a visiting yachtsman can enjoy a pleasant stay in a beautiful town without the difficulties of drying out against a rough sea wall.

Once upon a time, foolishly, I believed to paint the name of a home port on a yacht's stern was pretentious and somewhat similar to "my daughter is an honours student at Washington High" type of car bumper sticker. I was wrong. The home port name on a yacht stern stimulates the imagination of the interested passer-by. People on the quayside or the pontoon want to know where a yacht has come from. Not surprisingly perhaps, people have little care for local boats or local sailors. It is the distant mariners, visitors from somewhere thought to be exotic, which fuels their curiosity. Having the port name of Greenwich on Hobo's stern, encouraged people passing along the pontoon to say hello, to ask about my trip, spend a few friendly, and for me very precious, minutes, sharing a smile and offering me wishes for a safe voyage. So, in the future, the home port name will be on all the boats I sail.

*26 May – Day 19. Scarborough to Hartlepool, passage 41 nm, 8:29 hours*

When cruising on a yacht it is important to be flexible. The cruise itinerary and calendar are not proscribed and sailors should make decisions based on weather and tides. I had hoped to visit Whitby but the weather now intervened. The Met Office forecast suggested a gale was due the following day with northerly winds. The almanac clearly stated entry and exit of Whitby harbour shouldn't be attempted in strong northerly winds and that a difficult swell would probably persist for several days. If I held to my plan and visited Whitby, it was highly likely I would be stuck there. In addition to this frustrating prospect I was expecting crew. My friend Rebecca Scott from Greenwich Yacht Club was driving all the way from London to Yorkshire and I really wanted to offer her more of a sail than just a quick hop around the headland to Whitby. So my plan was changed, and when she arrived, we agreed Hartlepool as being a better destination, given the expectation of deteriorating weather.

At 10:57 we left Scarborough Harbour for the straightforward trip along the coast of North Yorkshire. After rounding Scarborough Rock the coast runs approximately to the north with few, if any, hazards for yachtsmen. The light northeasterly wind meant cold air but a full mainsail and working jib. By 15:00 we were off the dramatic ruins of Whitby Abbey and the conspicuous white piers of the town harbour. Though disappointed not to be sailing into this picturesque historic town, from our position offshore, it was easy to see how the entrance would be open to northerly and northeasterly winds and any seas rolling all the way down from the Artic.

At this halfway point in our passage the wind freshened and veered into the south pushing us forwards. By 17:50

we were off Redcar and the Salt Scar cardinal buoy. The industrial sprawl of Middlesbrough and Teesport lay to the west and we had to watch carefully and avoid the heavy shipping making its way to and from the River Tees. All that remained was to close in on Hartlepool and identify the entrance to Victoria Harbour. The almanac suggested a call to the Teesport harbour control on VHF radio channel 14 was necessary. However, our experience showed Teesport radio merely refers all yachtsmen to the private moorings at the all-tide Kafiga Landings. We arrived at 19:27 and quickly found a space, bows to the pontoon. Unfortunately, although Kafiga appears to be ideal for those sailors intending a visit to the old town, in reality, the pontoon is owned and run by local boat owners who have erected a solid, high security gate to the town which is padlocked out of club hours. So, as the tide wouldn't yet allow our entry to the huge and nearby Hartlepool Marina, we had dinner and warmed up after our eight and half hour passage. A VHF radio call to the marina staff suggested there would be enough water to enter the lock at 22:00. Despite there being an impressive 5 metres of water in the marina, the dredged entry channel through the west harbour has been neglected and Hobo's depth sounder only showed 1.9 metres of water three hours after low-water neaps. Fortunately the lock approach was well lit with a pontoon on the port side. So our entry was smooth and the staff were welcoming.

*27 – 30 May. Days 20 – 23*

This proved to be my first day truly storm bound, with Hobo tied to a pontoon in the quite stately 500 berth Hartlepool Marina. The gale pushed Hobo around as if we were rubbish in an alley. We tipped and swayed while the bangs and knocks of rope against metal provided a percussive soundtrack to the wind. The forces unleashed by the low pressure system were a timely frightening reminder – don't allow yourself to get caught out at sea in a gale.

Hartlepool Marina is one of those absurd monuments to the English quixotic nature. This is a truly huge Victorian ship dock, built to service the merchant shipping fleet in the nineteenth century, then taking our finished manufactured goods to the markets of the world. Some time last century, the British allowed these markets to be taken over by other emerging nations, and we gave up our trade and most of the wonderful red flagged merchant ships that used to be seen in ports across the globe. Consequently Hartlepool dock was no longer viable and was left neglected by the politicians of local government who should have known better. However, recently, a new regional development agency made the decision to, at last, reuse the wonderful dock for the establishment of a 500 berth marina. However, this is huge capacity and it appears the northeast region doesn't really need a 500 berth marina. A sailor entering from the sea may notice two things. Firstly, the marina is large enough for a yacht to need the GPS chart plotter to navigate around it and secondly, only about half the pontoon berths are occupied. Varieties of lichen have already colonised the wooden pontoons since the last footfalls of deck shoes, and seagulls, rather than sailors, roost, digesting meals of mussels, later to relieve themselves of the digestive waste. The marina is superb, but only through development agency tax payer subsidy can this harbour continue to meet its costs. However, while it lasts, Hartlepool marina is a great refuge for tired sailors on their way up or down the east coast.

On exploring the town of Hartlepool, I noticed something peculiar had happened since leaving Scarborough. The regional spoken accent had changed, and in just a mere

41 miles, the sound and style of speech had flipped from broad Yorkshire to musical Geordie. The mystery for me was how in this electronic media dominated age, in just 41 miles, English people can maintain two distinctly different dialects. There's tribalism here and something that perhaps has its roots in the people who invaded and settled these island shores during the mid-first millennium.

Meanwhile the gale, and its violent effect on the sea, continued, so after crew Rebecca left, I needed to find something to occupy my time. As I'd missed the famous Whitby due to the impending change in the weather, I decided a bus trip to the town would be a good substitute. This was cruising by bus. Public transport outside London, of course, exists, but, for a person used to the grand metropolis, the northeast network of routes was sometimes quite hard to understand. However, the marina office helped and after one slow bus to Middlesbrough and an even slower bus from there to Whitby, I arrived and found the town was in bank holiday mood. Whitby was full of day trippers determined to enjoy their holiday despite the weather. A priority for me was a walk to the harbour entrance to confirm the almanac guidance, namely, don't attempt to enter or leave in a strong northerly wind. The almanac advice was correct and I witnessed the frightening sea, white and rolling, powering its way between the piers and into the outer harbour.

Whitby's streets are pleasantly narrow but, to my taste, uncomfortably lined with shops selling mostly predictable touristy fare and the occasional Goth influenced gift shop – Bram Stoker and the Whitby episodes in his book *Dracula* has much to answer for. Apart from the river, the feature which almost dominates the town is the headland, topped by the remains of the circa seventh-century abbey. This is a must for any visitor. Unfortunately for me, English

Heritage had got there first and the newly built visitor centre, plus bank holiday entertainment provided by the Sealed Knot Society, in the corporate opinion of English Heritage, allowed them to demand a £4.50 per person entrance charge. This fee was levied to permit a visitor to walk through an old ruined building which, for at least the last six centuries, had been freely open to sheep, moles and we the public. I declined to pay what I considered to be a tax. To pay for the Disneyesque perversion of a ruined abbey was against my principles.

Walking the streets of Whitby I got the impression that, for the local tourist industry, real history, namely that of Saint Hilda and her abbey founded in 657 AD, the important Synod that in 664 settled the date of Christian Easter, and the later destruction of the abbey by the Norse raiders, was almost ignored. This abbey with its dramatic scenery and unique history appears to be missing from much of the Whitby tourist advertising. Saint Hilda and her abbey are fundamental to the history of Christianity in the UK and, consequently, integral to the development of the English Nation and later the British character, subsequently responsible for creating the largest Christian empire the world has known. For the civic leaders of Whitby to underplay this heritage is short sighted. It is as daft as suggesting the cities of Rome or Jerusalem should sidestep their religious history in favour of a more mundane and safe "plastic" story. Surely Whitby's civic leaders should now reopen the book, written by the Venerable Bede, and celebrate the abbey and Abbess Hilda, and promote both as Whitby's unique selling point?

The next day it rained and blew and the air temperature was at just 10 degrees Celsius. This was just too cold to sit on a boat in any comfort. The damp made it worse and, while I had chosen the correct direction for the bow in the easterly wind, now the wind was back to the west and the spray hood and companionway were decidedly in the line of fire. The weather pressure chart in the newspaper looked more like a page from the illustrated version of Revelations. Was someone or something trying to punish me? Being on the boat was miserable. Back in April, when I had contemplated the cruise, I assumed that I would need shorts and lashings of factor 50 sun block cream. I anticipated evenings sitting in the cockpit, eating dinner alfresco, and taking morning breakfast while bathed in early sunshine. But this summer was not like the summer I expected. After 23 days on board it was now time to accept reality and I went forth and bought an electric fan heater. For just £12.95, this heater plugged into shore power – cost £1.50 per day – allowed the boat to dry out and allowed me to feel a little more human.

Potentially what might be a dangerous subject but, one which I feel is open to journalistic reflection, are the native Geordies of Hartlepool, a people part descended from the numerous celtic tribes that once faced the Roman legions. My superficial impression of the area, formed after four days and largely based on visual data, is of soulless shopping centres and streets full of boys smeared in hair gel, wearing baggy nylon shell suits and trainers and, perhaps, proud to be descendants of the notorious, if comic, "monkey hangers" of 1805. The local Geordie girls appeared to be dressed by Ann Summers and look determined to attract the attention of the boys. As an anecdote of Gordie youth "culture", while on a quest for an electric power cable to enable me to use my fan heater, in frustration, I asked four girls for directions to a shop. After we collectively agreed that the nearest Halfords was too far away for a pedestrian, I noticed that one of these, perhaps thirteen-year-olds, had her hand stuffed inside a condom and was happily playing "glove puppets". Difficult to ignore, but in today's morally confused and politically correct society, perhaps something a mature single male could not safely comment upon. So, after four days in Hartlepool, I was disappointed to determine that the musical quality of the Geordie accent, whilst strangely attractive, was perhaps the only surviving aspect of the once proud local culture that I could detect. Unfortunately, my impression was that today's Geordies may have lost the essence of healthy community tradition. and now merely display an addiction to what, personally, I judge to be shoddy modern materialism.

But back to things maritime. Prior to this cruise I thought that, on the sea in a sailing boat, the disposable wheelie waste bin world of the land could be forgotten. Unfortunately not. Land dwellers are dirty, careless folk and their waste, so much a symbol of the late twentieth century, blows into the rivers and seas and in my location, the marinas. After the three days in Hartlepool, awaiting the gale to pass, I awoke at 04:00 and set off in Hobo, locking out of the marina an hour later. As I exited the lock gates, I was very pleased with myself to be on schedule and about to add another thirty nautical miles to my tally, but, suddenly, the engine slowed and boat speed dropped. My heart sank as I feared this might be the result of the diesel fuel bug problem returning. But whatever the cause, I quickly realised I needed to get some sail up or lose steerage altogether in the shallow and very narrow channel. With the jib rapidly hoisted and some forward movement achieved another thought passed through my mind. Perhaps the propeller had been fouled. I tried moving the gear lever alternatively ahead and astern but this failed to solve the problem. The engine revolutions remained low and clearly a six-hour sea passage was not a safe idea. I quickly called the lock keeper on the VHF radio and communicated my intention to immediately return to the marina under sail. The lock gates were reset and reopened and I slowly, oh so slowly, sailed Hobo back alongside a pontoon.

Once on the other side of the lock and with the boat secured in the marina, I considered the problem and remembered, over the last few days, I had spotted several plastic bags floating in the marina water but no waste skimmer craft in use. Perhaps it was not the fuel bug causing the engine problem, but a plastic bag fouling the two bladed folding prop. After a few jabs under the hull with the boat hook, small tell-tale pieces of plastic were removed and at least I now knew what I was up against. The curse of the supermarket had defeated my sailing plans. That a thin plastic bag can stop a ten horsepower diesel engine functioning is proof, if proof was needed, that this so-called convenience is really an environmental disaster. I could suggest that, in a truly civilised society, plastic bags be outlawed, and we would all return to using paper for our shopping. The solution to the problem of waste plastic bags is this simple.

Where there is one problem others soon follow. The boat yard workers started at eight o'clock but the manager who could authorise their activity didn't arrive until nine so I had to wait. There were, of course, three ways to shake the embrace of the plastic monster; moving the gear lever repeatedly between ahead and astern and the bag might be shaken free – however, I had already tried this to no avail; lift the boat out of the water by slipway hoist or crane and then remove the plastic; careen the boat over by attaching the main halyard to the pontoon and then from a dinghy stretch under the boat to reach the prop. There was a fourth that involved a snorkel, mask and swimming. Not surprisingly my preferred option was to have the marina management authorise a gratis lift by slipway hoist. After all, the plastic bag that had disabled and endangered Hobo, was left floating in their lock. Happily, the marina management arranged for Hobo to be towed to the slipway and lifted out. The remains of a large plastic bag were removed and although I had now lost 24 hours, all was set for a departure the next day. That evening Heather Criggie, my new crew, arrived.

*31 May – Day 24. Hartlepool to Amble. Passage 47 nm, 7:30 hours*

A bright early summer morning and the Met Office forecast was for a southeasterly wind force 3-4 but with the possibility of poor visibility. Nervously, following my experience of the previous day, at 05:50 we locked out of the marina and after clearing the outer harbour, turned on to a course of 340 degrees, a direction we would hold for the next forty or so nautical miles. The sun gradually warmed the air and a southerly breeze helped move Hobo up along the seemingly featureless coast of County Durham. First off the port beam came the town of Seaham and then the bold harbour piers of both Sunderland and Tynemouth. By 11:00 it was wind turbines off Blyth. While the sunshine was glorious and long overdue, the fickle breeze frequently required we resort to engine but after so many days harbour bound it was lovely to be at sea again. Just before reaching the town of Amble we saw the first seal of the trip and several puffins, both probably occasional residents of the nearby, excitingly named, Coquet Island.

The entrance to the Coquet River – the name apparently a derivation of the Latin word red rather than reference to any tendency of local females – at Amble is narrow but, with only the Pan Bush shoal laying in wait for any ill-prepared yachtsman, I felt quite confident. In calm conditions it presented no difficulty, although once inside the river, the navigable channel proved to be very narrow. Deep keel yachts must keep well to port side on entry, almost hugging the south jetty and ignoring the seductive wide expanse of clear water to starboard. One must ignore the normal niceties of staying on the correct side of the channel as over to starboard is just a thin layer of water over oodles of flat sand. The entrance to the marina is between piles and over a sill that, thankfully, has a well marked depth gauge. At 13:55, after an uneventful passage, we secured alongside a pontoon finger and settled down to enjoy this delightful Northumberland – the very name for a southerner suggests I was on the edge of England – village and the well managed, if expensive, marina.

*1 June – Day 25. Amble to Eyemouth. Passage 43 nm, 10:10 hours*

The first of June would appear to be a date full of summer magic. After twenty-five days of what felt like mostly miserable weather, I had now traversed the east of England, and ahead lay the picturesque Farne Islands and the mystical Lindisfarne. If further significance was needed, Scotland was our destination at nightfall. Unfortunately, as perhaps so often happens, the forces of nature had a surprise for me. At 04:00 rather than Homer's very poetic 'Dawn appearing fresh rosy-fingered' a damp shroud of fog lay over the river. The fog was thick enough to hide the river mouth and even the exit from the marina and, therefore, thick enough to be a serious problem for yachtsmen. The 05:20 Met Office shipping forecast for Tyne and Forth was for southeasterly wind, force 3-4 occasionally 5 later, and fog patches. Having planned for an early departure, dictated partly by the distance to our destination but more particularly by the need to exit the marina before the falling tide and sill barred our escape, our dilemma was how long to wait before we abandoned our sailing plan.

Having crew join the boat brings relief but also pressure for a skipper. If conditions are good, having crew helps sail the boat and offers companionship and amusement. However, when the weather conditions are borderline, a crew brings with them, responsibility. The skipper has to make decisions that will affect the enjoyment and safety of people other than himself. Also, there is the issue of expectancy. The crew travels to the boat expecting to go sailing. The pressure is on the skipper to provide sailing and not to "wuss out" due to being overly cautious. So, whereas if I had been sailing solo and confronted by fog I might have said to myself, "oh well I'll wait until tomorrow", as I had crew I felt the need to respond differently. Privately reluctant, but publicly confident, I therefore had Heather prepare Hobo for sea but still awaited the fog to lift. I was tense as I watched the clock tick closer to the time when exit from the marina would become impossible for another six hours.

Being a sailor used only to the south coast of England, for me, early morning fog in midsummer was something that burned off as the sun rose higher in the sky. The fog on the south coast is, more often than not, just mist and it blows away by mid-morning. With this, my south coast experience, and the fact that I noticed several other local yachts leaving the marina, at 07:00, literally as the sill depth gauge showed just 1.9 metres clearance, we rushed Hobo out into the river and left Amble.

To me the fog appeared to be lifting and I reasonably surmised we could, if unfortunately this situation changed, always return to Amble with the afternoon tide. The river's ebb at Amble produced a swell between the harbour piers and the depth sounder flickered up some horribly low numbers. However, real depth or just a disturbance caused by the swell, nevertheless we cleared the sand bar and turned to the north. As is the nature of poor visibility, as soon as the hard features of the harbour walls were behind us, the open sea with its fog appeared visually to be a blank white curtain and ghostly. A yacht directly ahead provided an aid for focus and something to gauge distance by, but the conditions were unsafe. Following the shore depth contours would ensure we stayed away from large shipping, but I was unhappy to continue further. The solution to the problem was to anchor in the bay and await the expected improvement in visibility. At 08:04 we anchored in five metres of water just off the beach at Alnmouth and waited. The boat rolled and mist swirled, lifted, fell and generally played games, so the decision to continue our passage to Eyemouth, or return with the afternoon tide to Amble, was not simple. However, at 10:00 I adjudged the visibility had improved enough, although fog banks could be seen at a distance moving on the breeze.

With a little sunshine, some breeze and some fog we hoisted sail and hugged the coast northwards towards Scotland – crew Heather's homeland. From studying the chart we gained the impression that the Northumberland coast is very scenic. Sadly, we only saw one of the many castles, something sounding Shakespearean, named Dunstanburgh. The fog returned and seemed to follow us as we started the process of buoy hopping – moving from one channel buoy to the next – taking the route inside the Farne Islands and close inshore along the east side of Holy Island. I had programmed the location of each buoy from Newton via Swedman to Plough Rock into the GPS chart plotter and it was only by piloting our way along this electronic dotted line we were able to navigate, what in strong winds would have been a hazardous course.

At 11:30 we briefly sighted Bamburgh Castle but that was it. The fog hid all sight of the apparently beautiful Farne Islands and Lindisfarne. It was at 13:50 we rounded Plough Rock cardinal and, with a now fresh southeasterly wind, we set out to sail a reach from Emmanuel Head and the 16 nautical miles across Berwick Bay. As we moved further offshore the sea state changed and we were soon surfing down waves. While exciting, it was obvious, even without masthead speed instruments, the wind was strengthening and there was an increasing risk of involuntary gybes. It was at this moment I discovered my plucky crew's vision wasn't quite 20/20 and not up to clearly seeing the tiny wind direction indicator on top of Hobo's very tall mast.

During passage planning using the small chartlet of Eyemouth, it appeared to me to suggest the harbour was sheltered from southerly winds. I believed it would be necessary to sail northwards past the harbour, leaving the offshore Hurkars rocks to port, before then sharply rounding Hobo up and reaching back towards the wind to squeeze through the very narrow entrance. Not for the first or last time I was to discover my personal mental impression, constructed from a small two dimensional chart sketch, was, in reality, slightly less than adequate.

Of course, as always, arrival at a new port created anxiety just when one is most tired, and with the fog and the increasing sea state, I was becoming less than happy. While the distance to go was no more than ten nautical miles, I was becoming worried by what appeared to be the large patch of white on the horizon, exactly where I expected Eyemouth's Gunsgreen Point to be. These clouds of white spray were either Moby Dick enjoying a jacuzzi or the Hurkars rocks, a vicious reef – either guarding or attacking, depending on your state of mind – at the entrance to Eyemouth. To my increasing horror, with the then high tide, the southeasterly sea was breaking heavily on this reef making our arrival point appear very "spectacular" and something less than inviting.

After a tense cockpit briefing, crew Heather and I prepared our plan. We would easily gybe around the cardinal buoy off the Hurkars and then close reach towards the harbour entrance. The plan sounded good, and I think Heather believed me for a few minutes, but when we arrived, the size of the headland and distances all seemed to have somehow shrunk. There was no protection from the land to lesson the wind strength, and in Charlie Chaplin movie style double quick time, Hobo hurtled through the two-hundred metre gap between the Hurkars reef to port and the impressive waves breaking on the Luff Hard Rocks to starboard. The sails were hurriedly dropped and, much less dignified than normal, Hobo, veiled in flapping sail cloth, lurched through the sixteen metre wide gap in the harbour breakwaters.

The contrast between the then threatening marine world and the torpor of the town's harbour was surreal. I felt like an alien landing on Earth for the first time. At 17:00 we were tied alongside another yacht and, despite, or because of the fog and the breaking waves and a ten hour passage, it felt very good to have now reached Scotland.

*2 June – Day 26. Eyemouth, Borders*

My morning walk showed the fresh southeasterly wind still to be blowing and the Hurkars reef looked fierce. So it seemed a rest day would be a very good idea before attempting the passage across the wide Firth of Forth. That I was now in Scotland was confirmed by the choice of door lock code, 1745, for the harbour side shower block. At least the friendly harbour master seemed to find the code amusing. Of course, like all jokes, if explanation is needed, they fall a little flat. Unbeknown to me, apparently Scots commonly regard the date of the Jacobite armed rebellion against Scotland's union with England as significant, and something they want to joke about with visitors from south of the border. The English are sometimes praised for their sense of humour, so it is perhaps sad that most visitors to Eyemouth are unlikely to get the 1745 joke as this date is almost unrecognised in England – blame the education system. There was something else about Eyemouth even less amusing; from tourist office information I discovered that on a Friday in 1881, a sudden storm off the entrance to the town cost the lives 189 fishermen as they battled wind and waves to return to safety. A chilling thought when we considered our own Friday arrival through the reefs. Perhaps it was partly because of this revelation, Heather, my plucky Scottish crew of two days, then decided to jump ship and take the bus back home.

*3 June – Day 27. Eyemouth to Abroath. Passage 47 nm, 9:30 hours*

The weather forecast seemed to be a copy of the last few days, with poor visibility now a permanent feature. However, the many sea-miles in front of me and my desire to reach Inverness by midsummer, encouraged my departure from this border town. At 06:30 I left Eyemouth, although, in doing so, I had to wait inside the harbour to allow a returning trawler to squeeze through the narrow entrance – it was just too small for two boats to pass. The sea outside was calm and with just a light breeze filling the mainsail I motor sailed towards St Abb's Head and then out further into the Firth of Forth. I had expected to see a lot of shipping heading to and from Edinburgh, the Scottish capital, but other than one small freighter I was alone. Four hours later I had crossed the shipping lanes and was abeam of the Isle of May. My course of 335 degrees took Hobo directly from St Abb's Head to Fife Ness, as I choose to use this point as a turning mark, thereby confirming my position in case the promised poor visibility materialised. Unfortunately, the wind remained light and backed into the north. At 12:03 I passed close to North Carr cardinal and, with a freshening East breeze, I trimmed sails and reached across St Andrews Bay. Yet again the wind dropped, so it was back to motor sailing, but not for long. As the wind disappeared and an annoying swell rolled Hobo to and fro, the engine revolutions fell and the boat slowed. It appeared that the diesel fuel bug I believed I had destroyed, while in Burnham-on-Crouch, had merely been sleeping at the bottom of the fuel tank.

At this, the seven hour mark in the passage, the engine was comatose. Despite the large quantities of micro organism killer I had already used in the fuel tank, perhaps due to the swell, this MRSA super bug of the marine world had survived, and a quick inspection of the recently fitted clear fuel pipes showed a black, slug like, "alien being", camped between the tank and the primary filter. Even after removing this stowaway the low revs problem persisted, therefore, I had to remove the in-line strainer and poke out the blockage with a match stick. After I had re-primed and vented the system, the engine seemed happy and energetic after its minor thrombosis. I had a smile on my face, but playing mechanic on a marine engine is difficult enough while in harbour, but at sea, with the boat doing its impression of a routine for "strictly dancing", the challenge is formidable.

Through the mist I now steered the re-energised Hobo towards the shoreline. What, however, do you do, when after nine hours solo sailing, you approach a harbour that the almanac warns is dangerous to enter in southeasterly swell? That there was a southeasterly swell and poor visibility was fact. The question for a sailor arriving looking for a haven was, just how much of a southeasterly swell is dangerous? It is a dilemma and unless there is alternative nearby harbour facing another direction, reluctantly you have to just prepare a plan and try. Happily for me, the newly acquired GPS chart plotter again proved well worth the £450 purchase price. Its small glowing screen clearly indicated Hobo's position on the leading line and gradually the white harbour piers, complete with markers, materialised out of the misty grey gloom. Allowing for the following swell, I pointed Hobo for the small gap but as I got closer I was puzzled by the apparent bright red light directly ahead. Was this a warning signal that Abroath harbour was closed? It was my reoccurring day/nightmare that I would sail for 10 hours and arrive exhausted at a harbour and find it "closed". However, I was committed to entry, but, and as Hobo slewed herself between the piers, I noticed that the frightening red light was just a fisherman dressed in clothing with florescent red shoulder and chest stripe – very helpful. From the outer to the inner harbour and then through the gates, at 16:00 I was safely alongside in Arbroath's so-called wet dock.

*4 June – Day 28. Arbroath, Tayside*

Arbroath is a plain fishing town. I describe it as plain, not as an insult but as a description of architectural fact. The people here could have built houses which exploited the visual possibilities of its waterfront, but my impression was of quiet practicality rather than a celebration of beauty. The native property owners had not sought to decorate their buildings with frippery. This was my second Scottish fishing town, the first, Eyemouth, to me was surprising in having a stunning sandy cove where nearly all the houses defiantly faced away from the sea and perhaps the Scottish word dreich can be applied to both Eyemouth and Arbroath. Friendly people but dreich buildings.

There must be something about east coast fishing towns that results in strange failures in basic marketing. While in Grimsby fish docks, it seemed to me blindingly obvious that a visitor should find cafés and restaurants serving local fresh seafood. Now I was in Arbroath, famous to we southerners for its Smokies – a delicately smoked haddock much desired by epicureans everywhere. However, while Arbroath is certainly full of fish processors and takeaway fish and chip cafes, frustratingly I couldn't find anywhere offering to serve me a meal of Smokies. After searching the harbour side and many of the town's streets I found just one place – Café Seven, 124 the High Street – where I was able to enjoy a breakfast of Arbroath's finest. That we Britons seem so blind to the possibilities presented by our traditional local food, is bizarre. We have so much we could learn from our nearest continental cousins; not their acceptance of high taxation, short Emperors or penchant pour révolution of course, but their sensual and enthusiastic celebration of great regional food.

At last, the sun briefly broke through the cloud and the boat was a relaxing place to be. Jobs there were many, but even with problems thrown upon me by the wheel of life, this maritime world was somehow wholesome and far removed from the commuter's struggle. A sailing trip is a great personal journey rather than a mere cycle in the corporate/state process. Whereas commuters will tomorrow undergo the very same journey and trials, and again every tomorrow until redundancy, retirement or death, a mariner on a voyage will physically live each journey, a passage containing both trial and nirvana in equal measures.

*5 June – Day 29. Abroath to Aberdeen. Passage 55 nm, 11:30 hours*

The early morning Met Office forecast was for a northeasterly wind force 2 to 3 with occasionally poor visibility. My impression was the weather was becoming settled but, unfortunately, the wind was "settled" from the wrong direction – the northeast – not the direction I needed to sail north up the Scottish east coast. At 07:30 I guided Hobo out from the wet dock then through the inner and outer harbours and left Arbroath. Outside there was a short choppy sea and the wind was on the nose so I had to motor sail. With a distance of 55 sea miles to cover, beating into a short vigorous chop was not very attractive. It is in exactly these conditions that a large engine in a sailing yacht would repay the initial cost penalty. A twenty horsepower engine – twice the size of Hobo's – would have allowed the boat to punch through the sea and maintain hull speed though moving directly into the wind and waves. With the ten horse power engine fitted to Hobo I needed the extra push from the mainsail if I was to maintain four and a half knots and this, unfortunately, required steering a tacking course adding distance to my preferred rhumb line.

By adopting this motor sail and short tacking method, I was abeam Scurdie Ness, off Montrose, by 10:00 and then Todhead Point at 12:37. While there was weak sunshine, the northeasterly wind was very cold and stubbornly from the worst possible direction. Had the almanac not described Stonehaven as a town harbour, requiring deep keel yachts to dry out against the rough granite wall, I would have chosen to stop. It is at times like this the solo sailor has to grit his/her teeth and just persevere. It may not have been pleasant and motor sailing against the wind can be described in far harsher terms, but I was making progress north. After twenty-nine days I was starting to feel a profound need to get off this cold east coast. I felt I had to add as many miles as possible, while maintaining my day sail philosophy, so I chose to push on to Aberdeen.

Girdle Ness, marking the southern approach to Aberdeen harbour, lay ahead and I counted off what felt like several painful hours, before I was able to peer around at the entrance. At last, at 18:00, I was off the southern breakwater and able to call the harbour Vessel Traffic Service (VTS) and request their permission to enter.

Rather than receiving a cheery welcome, when contacted, the officer in charge of Aberdeen harbour kept me in a "hold position" for thirty minutes outside the southern breakwater, before finally authorising entry. For a solo sailor, being kept reaching back and forth in a small sea area, subject to both swell and backwash, is not the ideal way to finish a twelve hour passage. However, my official permission finally was received, I followed the VTS instructions and Hobo entered this Heathrow of Scottish ports, apparently an event rare enough for VTS to warn all other vessels of my presence.

However, the port of Aberdeen is interesting. It's a relatively small harbour when compared to Southampton or Portsmouth, but it is a harbour impressively full of oil support ships, those bizarre vessels with towering, impossible looking, superstructures at the bow and flat long after decks. Ships, ships, ships, with the VTS port radio – just like air traffic control – professionally managing all vessel movements.

When describing the harbour, the almanac is not encouraging to yachtsmen, suggesting that there are no facilities for non-commercial craft. However, Aberdeen is ideally positioned a little over half way between Arbroath and Peterhead so I was determined to use this, the safest port, for my passage up the Scottish coast. On a point of principle, I believe it important for yachtsmen to exercise their traditional rights and access any available all tide haven on an otherwise exposed coastline.

It is easy to presume a rich and major city like Aberdeen would welcome visiting yacht crews and want them to spend their pounds or other currency in local businesses. Unfortunately, this appeared not to be the case, as, while the harbour authorities did provide a berthing manager in a peaked cap to direct me to a space on Commercial Quay in Albert basin – a steel walled dockside in the underused fish wharf section of the harbour – there were none of the normal facilities. Not only was there no pontoon for Hobo or shower block for me, the harbour water was littered with floating rubbish and slicked with diesel. But the berthing of Hobo was accomplished and the friendly manager kindly offered me his own office shower to use.

With Hobo moored against a high blank wall in the tidal trawler harbour, leaving the boat unattended was not really advisable. Therefore, sadly, I didn't see Aberdeen, the Granite City. I didn't visit the shops or the restaurants. I didn't spend my money. I didn't get a chance. Aberdeen council, whilst I'm certain obsessed by the oil industry, should offer better facilities for non-commercial mariners. In a harbour of this size, a small corner could be easily allocated to leisure craft, and a floating pontoon provided, allowing yachtsmen to see the town and spend money boosting the local economy. The fact that the harbour authorities chose to levy the then near standard Scottish charge of £17 a night to moor Hobo in water that could be considered a serious health hazard, is yet another example of their negative attitude to non-commercial mariners. Yet the complaint having been made, I still think we yachtsmen, on a passage, should visit Aberdeen and assert our traditional right to a secure and safe refuge. Perhaps, on our behalf, organisations such as the Royal Yachting Association and Cruising Association should be lobbying Aberdeen harbour authorities and council to provide better facilities.

*6 June – Day 30. Aberdeen to Peterhead. Passage 25 nm, 4:40 hours*

Once again the Met Office predicted a northeast wind, but while the direction was disappointing, the strength was benign and the distance to Peterhead was a mere wee skip of 25 nautical miles. The fact that this distance allowed the passage to be completed within one favourable tide helped lift my slightly jaded spirit. It had been thirty days on the east coast and I now guessed the several reasons why perhaps I had not met or crossed the tracks of many cruising yachts. This day the temperature was 12 degrees Celsius and with the wind chill coming off the water you might understand what I, by then, considered to be the belligerent aspect of this so-called summer. I started imagining perhaps all this bad weather was located exclusively just above Hobo. In Bram Stoker's story *Dracula*, there is a schooner called the Demeter that has storm clouds and poor visibility constantly overhead, dogging its passage up the English east coast to Whitby. Yet Hobo was by then well past Whitby and there was no Transylvanian count with a blood fetish onboard and yet the accurst weather still appeared to be following me. A little bit of cabin fever perhaps.

To add to my confusion the British newspapers reported a new Met Office weather prediction of a hot summer with July and August possibly record breakers. The folk in the Met Office really should get out more.

At 07:30 I received permission from VTS to leave Aberdeen – immediately – so I quickly headed out into the bay to face the northeast breeze, substantially repeating the sailing of yesterday. Happily the favourable tide swept

Hobo northward along this hazard free piece of coastline. In a mere 4 hours Peterhead harbour was off the port bow and I approached the wonderful wide entrance, equally welcoming to both yachtsmen and commercial shipping.

In contrast to Aberdeen, the water quality here was excellent. Peterhead harbour is built around a large bay with movie *Local Hero* type sandy beach and lots of oil support ships. Whilst I praise the splendid harbour, sadly to my eye, the town is yet another example of the Scottish east coast lack of architectural flair. The town appeared bleak, almost dour and cheerless, another seaside community that perhaps, over the last two centuries, came to regard the sea as just an provider of economic advantage rather than a thing of beauty and pleasure.

Later in the day as I visited yet another branch of the Coop – Scotland's favourite supermarket? – I noted how in smaller towns the shelf space devoted to various types of alcohol and meat pies – some a sort of yellow and mysteriously named Bridies – is quite formidable enough to have any metropolitan nutritionist foaming at the mouth.

*7 June – Day 31. Peterhead to Buckie. Passage 51 nm, 8:00 hours*

In the morning the Met Office again repeated the now standard forecast, namely, a northerly wind with occasionally poor visibility. This had been the fifth day in a row with north to northeasterly winds. What cheered me was the fact that after a short beat north, I would be able to free off the sheets and reach Hobo west along the Moray Firth coast. At 07:10 I left the very pleasant Peterhead Marina and once more headed out into the north wind. I had planned my passage to round Rattery Head at slack water, close inshore. The almanac had warned of dangerous seas in heavy weather off this cornerstone of a headland and suggested 5 nautical miles was the safe offing. However, with the conditions, I believed the inshore route would be perfectly safe. But not for the first time or the last, as I approached the headland, I repeatedly peered through the binoculars at the horizon, searching for any breaking waves. Happily I found none and at 08:46 I was abeam the lighthouse and it was quite thrilling at last to be able to gradually alter course from north to west.

Knowing I had now reached north Scotland, a place that, when at home watching the TV news or looking at maps, always looked so far from London, I felt satisfaction and growing confidence. At 10:14 I passed the town of Fraserburgh and then occupied the time playing my usual "game" of identifying and marking off headlands on the chart. At 12:50 I was just north of Macduff and a rare sight, a ship, the Gemini Explorer research vessel I'd last seen in Aberdeen harbour, then passed Hobo on the port side. After so much solitude the friendly waving hands were much appreciated. At 16:00 I skirted the Middle and West Muck reefs to approach the harbour of Buckie on its leading line. Soon I was tied alongside a sad looking old schooner, clearly home to someone, but now gradually decaying in this largely disused fishing harbour.

Buckie harbour on the Moray Firth provided me with yet another example of missed opportunity on the East Coast. Buckie is roughly halfway between Peterhead and Inverness. It is a safe haven with access at all states of the tide. Inside the main pier heads there are four protected deep water harbour sections. However, there is a problem, deterring visiting yachtsmen, there isn't a wall-side pontoon. This means any yacht has to lay alongside the rough granite walls and, with the local tidal range, needs to set long warps and adjust their length periodically to protect the hull's top sides. Buckie's four deep water sections, on the day I visited, had just six commercial craft berthed with the rest of the harbour totally empty. All that would be needed to attract visiting yachts with smiling crews and heavy wallets to this small town would be to provide a visitor's pontoon placed on just one of the many walls. There would be no need to build a permanent expensive marina, just a pontoon able to rise and fall with the tide. From this pontoon yacht crews would be able to visit the town to shop, eat and drink, knowing their boats were safe. Buckie harbour side would once again have life and become the port of choice for cruising yachtsman heading to or from Inverness.

My east coast travail was almost over. The seemingly total absence of leisure craft had been disconcerting and I longed to sail with and cross the tracks of other mariners. The difference between sailing on the south coast and here on the east to me had been surprising. Another aspect of Scottish coastal waters I noted was the huge Scottish blue and white Saltires painted on the sides of many trawlers. It took me some time to surmise a reason for craft, not known for their expensive paint jobs, to allocate money for attention seeking decoration. My guess was the painted flags are used to evade the restrictions of the Merchant Shipping Act 1995, Article 4; you know, the one that concerns "carrying improper colours" on British shipping? The regulations state British ships must fly the British marine red ensign, not any cute local "nationalist" symbols, so trawlers skippers, perhaps, have decided to boldly paint their defiance on their hulls.

*8 June – Day 32. Buckie to Inverness. Passage 49 nm, 9:00 hours*

My plan had always been to use the Caledonian Canal to reach the west coast of Scotland, and with this pestilent non-summer and the persistent northerly winds I was all the more convinced this was the right decision. So as I planned the day's passage towards Inverness I drew my pencil lines on the paper chart.

The northerly airflow continued however, but thankfully the weather was settled enough for me to push onwards. At 07:10 I left Buckie harbour motoring into light drizzle and poor visibility. The compass heading had Hobo pointed across Spay Bay towards Halliman Skerries just north of Lossiemouth. At 09:25 I reached the most northerly latitude of my cruise at 57, 44 degrees North. Although only a third of the way around Britain, after six-hundred and sixty nautical miles, from this point on I would be moving southwards. To a solo sailor it felt like I was on my way home. I had a smile on my face from ear to ear and I indulged myself by recording the moment on my little digital camera.

What wind there had been then disappeared and from here I had to motor along the coast crossing Burghead Bay with views of the Cromarty Firth on the far eastern horizon. I was abeam Rift Bank South at 13:51 and then began the process of piloting Hobo through the various sandbanks festooned with their colonies of fat "black" seals.

Judging by my experience sailing British waters, seals are now more common than cod or wild salmon. It is a puzzle to this non-sentimental animal lover just why it is that we don't eat seal meat? We, well most of us anyway, eat cows, sheep, pigs and chickens, even wild fluffy rabbits and brown eyed deer. Why can't we eat seals? They are free-range and organic. From visual evidence seals are thriving and getting fat from eating the endangered fish stocks that the EU chauffeur driven droids of Brussels suggest must be conserved. So why doesn't the UK have a seal hunting season. Seal steak and chips anyone?

As I reached the impressive Fort George, built in 1769, I believe, to guard Protestant North Britain from the next assault from the sea or insurgency supported by the long time irritating and usually catholic French, the sun at last came out and, for what felt like the first time since I arrived in Scotland, a little bit of midsummer blazed down. At 14:31 from the narrows off Chanonry Point I steered south past the channel buoys Munlochy, Petty Bank and Middlebank to pass under famous Kessock Bridge at 15:45. Using the VHF radio I called ahead to Clachnaharry sea lock to advise them of my impending arrival. The in bound estuary current at this point in the Firth is very strong, so I held close to the southern shore to ensure Hobo wasn't swept past the canal lock entrance. At 16:02 I entered the sea lock with all boat fenders deployed and I relished the thought that ahead me lay several days of relatively stress free cruising – cruising where the continual tyranny of the weather forecast could largely be ignored. Two smiling lock keepers took my warps and without fuss or delay Hobo moved from salt to freshwater. Just one more lock and a swing bridge and I arrived at Seaport Marina, Inverness. After 32 days on the boat, to me this quiet arrival was like Dom Pérignon champagne to a race winner. There were no crowds or applause as I stepped on to the pontoon but inside my chest I felt a huge smile and I could have hugged any female generous enough to allow me inside a barge pole distance.

*The Caledonian Canal*

At this point in my story I feel the need to ask the reader for forgiveness for repetition. Lock and Loch will occur frequently as will Lough when I reach the island of Ireland. It appears the word "Loch" is from the language of the Gaels who settled and conquered what we now call Scotland from the late fifth century. Unfortunately, of course, the Gaels didn't have a word for a man made twin gated water machine invented to raise and lower boats, so we are stuck with its English name. So it's Locks and Lochs from here on.

This fifty nautical mile canal is simply wonderful. It is a practical waterway that allows marine craft to move from one Scottish coast to another avoiding the cost and difficulty presented by the most northern Pentland Firth route. That the north coast route takes longer, will cost more in diesel and overnight berthing and is potentially more dangerous, is borne out by the fact that in the year 1822 it was considered cost-effective to the canal builders to complete this superb piece of Victorian civil engineering. Yet the practical advantages are only part of the reason for choosing to use the Caledonian Canal. The Great Glen, through which the canal passes, is very beautiful. A seagoing craft can sail or motor the twenty-eight nautical miles of the four lochs that, together with the twenty-two nautical miles of constructed canal, make up the route through the Highlands. One of these lochs is, of course, the fabled Loch Ness – the largest expanse of freshwater in Britain.

The principal practicalities of using the Caledonian Canal are that a yacht of less than 4.11 metre draft can make the passage, coast to coast, in 2½ days and with the mast up. During the passage a yacht will use twenty-nine locks and pass through ten swing bridges – all operated by British Waterway staff. Each lock, on average, will take thirty minutes to transit.

The canal was engineered by Thomas Telford between 1803 and 1822 and cost the then British Tax Payer £905,258 – over twice the original estimate and although nearly impossible to equate at today's value, I assume a vast amount of money. However, Telford's achievement was recognized internationally and he subsequently helped engineer the 118 mile long Göta Canal for the then Swedish King.

A short-term transit licence to use the canal can be bought at either end and its eight day duration includes overnight berthing and the use of showers et cetera. Any crew choosing to use all the opportunity presented to explore the lochs, enjoy forest walks and the nearby Ben Nevis, would, I believe, find the inclusive fee very good value.

This is the good news about the Caledonian Canal, but naturally there are things that could be improved. While the wild lochs are the sublime part of the adventure, they also represent the biggest missed opportunity. Somehow the canal administration has focused all their attention on the man-made canal sections. It is on the constructed canal that one finds the vast majority of overnight moorings, facilities and restaurants. On the four lochs there is almost nothing but water and scenery. While this complaint may be considered crass by some, beauty is nothing if it cannot be seen and enjoyed unhurried. The almost total lack of mooring facilities on the lochs result in yachts being forced, almost like car drivers on a motorway, to pass quickly through the picturesque natural scenery to find a safe overnight berth on the man-made canal at either end. As an example, according to the official British Waterways map of Loch Ness, this thirty-five square miles of water offered only three public moorings. This is bizarre. While some might claim this lack of moorings is in the name of so-called conservation, thirty-five square miles of beautiful scenery deserves to be seen s.l.o.w.l.y. To spend at least one night moored on Loch Ness is a must for any yachtsman. Either British Waterways or the Highlands Council should provide many more public overnight moorings on the lochs. This would encourage yachts using the canal to stay in the Highland area longer and more time spent would result is a boost to the local economy.

Having, on a previous sailing holiday, passed through the Göta Canal in Sweden I feel qualified to comment on another small aspect of the canal management which could be improved. In addition to providing many more overnight moorings on the lochs, the Swedish type of lock and bridge signals could also be adopted. On the Göta Canal there are traffic lights beside each lock and bridge. On arrival a yacht will see a red light. When the lock or bridge keeper has noted the yacht's presence, an amber or white light will flash. When the gates are in the process of opening and entry permitted, a green light is displayed. All very simple. Without a traffic light system a yacht transiting the Caledonian canal's twenty-nine locks and ten bridges may have to contact each keeper via the VHF radio – most don't answer or delight in being cryptic about when they will open the lock or bridge. Without confirmation of if and when keeper intends to open, it is sometimes necessary to tie up a yacht and leave the boat purely to walk to the office to learn when the lock or bridge will move. The Swedish simple light system as used on Göta Canal would improve the situation for all canal users.

While the canal itself equals the splendour of the Swedish Göta – also partly the work of Telford – the modern management of the Caledonian doesn't quite live up to the previously high Victorian standards. While some lock keepers are energetic, that is, happy to work at helping vessels pass through the locks, others appeared disinterested, and like too many British employees, only prepared to take part in the minimum of process. At a well-tended lock, keepers greet the vessel and take warps ensuring each boat is correctly moored. When the water is raised or lowered the keeper of the well-tended lock will occasionally check that the crew and the boat are safe and all is well. When the process is complete and the gates open, the staff return the warps to the crew and ask where they are bound and perhaps offer advice on the best overnight stops. At the slovenly managed lock, when the gates open the staff ignore the craft entering or leaving forcing them to fend for themselves. As the water swirls lock keepers chat to each other – about who knows what – but they are careless about the boats in the lock and their crews. For the canal user the difference is profound. The former is fun, sociable and reassuring. The latter, hard work and stressful.

But these observations aside, the canal is truly a wonderful construction. Rather than London's Millennium Dome of plastic fabric or another glass and steel girder office block, 19th-century Brits chose to boost the national economy by building something vast, useful, and still creating wonder more than two hundred years later. Thomas Telford, the engineer, had the vision and drive necessary to link the four natural Scottish lochs into a top-class waterway. I salute him.

*9 June – Day 33. Seaport, Caledonian Canal, Inverness*
Having now reached the vibrant confident Highland city of

Inverness, the contrast between this and what I felt to be the gloomy east coast Scottish towns became even more apparent. The grey and dour architecture of Eyemouth, Arbroath, Aberdeen, Peterhead and Buckie was disappointing, but with Inverness I had returned to the architectural norm I believe suggests a celebration of life. In Inverness, there are trees planted beside the river and the roadways. Here houses have exterior features, not just practical, but added to the sake of beauty. Houses, in some cases, have painted masonry and the town is visually exciting. Compared to the East Coast ports where grey is the dominant colour and paint seems a rare commodity, Inverness is a return to the conspicuously healthy and definitely more wealthy. Along with all the normal excitement of a high-street area well-managed, importantly for sailors, Inverness has two yacht chandlers stocking all the overpriced boaty items every craft requires to stay in top condition. As I had decided to treat myself to a rest day, the chandlers supplied equipment necessary for me to service the engine. Ahead of a three-day passage through canals, lochs and locks I wanted to be sure the engine was bonnie and strong. Also, later on this day my Scottish crew returned. The appropriately named Heather, who had jumped ship at Eyemouth, now bravely returned to help Hobo through the locks.

*10 June – Day 34. Seaport to Urquhart Bay, Loch Ness. Passage 14 nm*

To exit the harbour basin at Seaport one has to "book" a place with the lock keepers. The small stair of locks and the road bridge can be busy and of course the early morning Scottish "rush" needs to be considered. The night before I had supplied the lock keeper with Hobo's details and at the first opening of the morning we joined three other boats for the lift up the three Muirtown locks. From the top of the locks the canal skirted the west side of Inverness and here a little bit of local culture blew in towards Hobo from the towpath. There was the sound of a solitary piper, probably forced out of his home at dirk point by his wife or partner, to then wander zombie-like beside the canal, practising his frightening instrument of audio torment. Over the next two weeks I was to become accustomed to encountering these seemingly exiled pipers, wandering far from home, like old testament lepers, or pariahs from a strange cult.

Even allowing one hour for our lunch it took a mere four hours to reach the beginning of Loch Ness, the home of the fabled monster Nessie. The Loch is a beautiful, long, very deep, stretch of fresh water, darkly profound and with shores undeveloped to an almost neglected level. While the natural beauty is worthy of conservation – beauty not seen by people is merely an academic proclamation. Loch Ness on this Sunday afternoon in the middle of June was almost a boat free zone. I observed a mere trickle of craft motoring quickly towards the northern exit to the canal; just four rental cruisers their crews looking forlorn and confused, plus two large passenger trip boats "monster hunting". Nothing else. Granted the weather was disappointingly Scottish, that is only 14 degrees Celsius, with a threatening sky and the tops of the tree-lined hills hidden by low cloud and mist, but this was a Sunday in summer. Where were all the hardy Scots? It is hard to believe that something so famous and so beautiful should be so empty and so under used. That Loch Ness, this 20 mile lake, offers very few visitor moorings would appear to be part of the problem.

My personal expectation was for a quiet idyllic evening spent watching the sun set below the hills, observing the birds and animals preparing for their dinner and enjoying the gloaming. Unfortunately, the only visitor boat mooring sheltered from the northeast wind was at Dores and the annual "Rock Ness" waterside pop festival was in full bass blast. My search elsewhere for orange or yellow visitor buoys was in vain. The only mooring I found was at Urquhart bay, in 8.5 metres of water – a less than idyllic anchorage, where the road noise and the northeast wind meant the evening was an in cabin affair. Loch Ness is huge and a national – and by that I mean British – treasure. For the nation of currently sixty-two million citizens to fully enjoy its natural beauty, leisure craft need far more opportunity to stop and allow their crews to relax. Perhaps when there are plentiful moorings the loch will look less abandoned and monsterish. Perhaps when "cheery wee" boats are able to play upon its waters, Loch Ness will truly be beautiful and at peace.

*11 June – Day 35. Loch Ness to Great Glen Water Park. Passage 22 nm*

So a night was spent on the Loch. The early morning mist was atmospheric and the still waters reflected the beautiful ruin of Urquhart Castle. My usual mug of tea and chocolate biscuit were consumed slowly as I mentally consumed and absorbed the fluid vista. With great reluctance I broke the hypnotic natural silence by turning the key to the engine and at 07:44 we let the mooring buoy go and slowly motored out of the bay heading southwest towards Fort Augustus.

The loch side is as under used by Scots as the water. Clearly, the Highlands, are not a favourite place for Scottish nationals and no-one should try blame the infamous "highland clearance". Whereas a lake this size in Sweden, Switzerland or Italy would have small cosy settlements and villas dotted around its perimeter and slopes, complete with stately lake steamers delivering mail and people to wooden jetties, Loch Ness is a people free zone. Almost no-one lives on either bank of the loch.

Three hours after leaving Urquhart Bay we approached

the swing bridge at Fort Augustus and, as the lock keepers declined to answer our call on the VHF radio, we tied Hobo up against the long pontoon on the north bank. Fort Augustus has a stair of five locks and well maintained pontoons both before and after the locks allowing craft to moor and explore the cafés, pubs and restaurants that trade at this highlands crossroad. Souvenir hats, T shirts and postcards, all emblazoned with the monster brand were on sale but what to me appeared significant was that, one of the lockkeepers was heard to comment to a tourist "we in Scotland owe visitors to Loch Ness so much but offer so little".

It took just less than 1½ hours to transit the five Fort Augustus locks and raise Hobo 12 metres higher. Just another two locks and then out on to the 4 mile long, but shallow Loch Oich, at 32.3 metres above sea level, the highest point on the Caledonian Canal. The passage channel through the loch is marked by buoys but the shallows off Glengarry and Port MacDonell are a little confusing. Slow ahead was certainly the sensible choice.

At the western end of the Loch is the Great Glen Water Park, a small "time share" holiday centre. The pontoons and club house in a rural setting provide a relatively rare opportunity for yachtsmen seeking somewhere for more than just a single night stay. It would no doubt be particularly suitable for those families with children onboard. It had taken us just 4¾ hours, excluding a stop for lunch, to travel the 22 nautical miles from Urquhart Bay.

*12 June – Day 36. Great Glen Water Park to Corpach. Passage 17 nm*

The nearby Invergarry and Port MacDonnell on Loch Oich deserve special note for it was hereabouts that, sometime after the year 1727, there was the first sighting of another loch "monster", the kilt. Curiously, today it is one of the recognised symbols of all Scotland. A Lancashire industrialist and English Quaker Thomas Rawlinson came to Glengarry to secure timber to fuel his foundry furnaces. His local Highland employees needed suitable work clothes and, with the help of a British Army tailor stationed at Inverness, the short pleated kilt was devised from the locally worn long and belted plaid. Worn at Glengarry by Thomas Rawlinson and his patron, Ian, the chief of the MacDonnell clan, the short kilt was later adopted and popularised in the nineteenth century by novelist Sir Walter Scott and the many Scottish regiments of the British Army. The rest, as some may claim, "is history".

The northerly air still flowed south from the Artic and while it wasn't raining, this definitely did not feel like summer. Having accepted the reality that the Caledonian Canal is less of a leisurely cruising area than a picturesque coast to coast "motorway", we rose betimes and at 08:20 set off to the west. After the Laggan swing bridge there was just one more barrier before we entered the fourth and final loch. Sadly it appears the Highlander folk had other things to do than create romantic names for expanses of water; we left the lock and entered Loch Lochy. A fresh following wind now hurtled us along the deserted, dare I call it lake? We achieved 6.8 knots over the ground – not bad for a 30 foot yacht – and in just under an hour and a quarter we were at Gairlochy. Just 7½ miles further along the canal and we arrived at the top of Neptune's Staircase otherwise know as Banavie. The top of the "staircase" is the recommended place for an overnight stay for a yacht bound either east or west due to the number of convenient pubs close by although, of course, I failed to learn this useful fact until later.

While to the south the view was of the scenic splendour of Britain's highest mountain, the snow capped Ben Nevis, almost directly below us lay Loch Linnhe – west coast salt water. Between Hobo and the canal exit point was a drop of 19.5 meters, achieved via eight locks. The lock keepers here were excellent and all eight locks were completed in little more than an hour. Just one more set of wooden gates and at 15:50 we arrived at Corpach sea lock, the coast to coast Caledonian Canal completed. It had taken Hobo 19:55 hours over a three day period to achieve the 54 nautical mile passage.

*13 June – Day 37. Corpach to Kerrera. Passage 30 nm, 5:30 hours*

The islands of the Inner Hebrides awaited us and despite enjoying the relatively relaxed nature of canal cruising I was keen to be at sea once more. Added to this was the emotive magnetism of heading home. Not so much for the sofa and warm bedroom but the intangible hunger to complete my voyage and sail back up the Thames. I'd achieved the east coast passage and crossed Scotland and Hobo was now firmly pointed southward. However, the weather forecast was again discouraging – strong northeasterly wind, drizzle and poor visibility. But here's the other non-scenic beauty of sailing the Hebrides and the Firth of Clyde area; the islands are so numerous and lochs so narrow as to ensure that despite the strong wind, the seas are calm and a well reefed yacht can be sailed safely and in relative comfort.

At 08:50 we locked out of Corpach and took the ebb tide down Loch Linnhe. There was a cold, squally wind blowing off the slopes of Ben Nevis and several layers of fibre pile clothing were applied to small bodies. Two comic impressions of Mr Blobby enthusiastically bounced over the deck having found competition against a German flagged Hallberg-Rassy yacht. After the solitude of the east coast, sailing with/against another yacht was, to me, the racing man, great fun. To paraphrase poet Lord Alfred Tennyson, "rocks to right of them, rocks to left of them, rocks in front of them, Boldly they rode and well, Into the jaws of Death, Into the mouth of Hell". Not quite hell, of course, but the narrowness of the loch compared with the vast featureless watery expanse of the east coast was something quite new to me and a little unnerving. Hobo raced on under full sail with both wind and current and the 8 nautical mile loch was soon completed.

Corran Narrows with its ferry boat lay directly in our path. A quick side step to port and we avoided the hazard. By then I started to realise that navigation in the Inner Hebrides was to be all island counting and headland identification. Quite fun really and a matter of pencil marking on the chart each physical land feature as we passed by. However, forgetting to tick off created problems as in poor light each island looked the same. Here the navigation required was more like hill walking than sailing.

At Shuna Isle we turned to port and passed through the narrow straight at Port Appin, a little more than ¼ nautical mile wide. It was near to this point I noted there was another difference between the Scottish east coast and the Hebrides. Here the sea charts are decorated with strange Gael place names that defy pronunciation by we Sassenachs. We had just passed Rubh' Aird Ghainimh to starboard and to port there was Dearg Sgeir. While I understand I'm in danger of provoking those in the politically correct "lets rush culturally backwards" brigade, I wonder how any sailors not fluent in Gaelic – surely, the vast majority – would describe his/her position if in an emergency Mayday situation. I twice pity the sailor using the VHF radio to make a distress call, "Help me I'm sinking off Rubh' Aird Ghainimh".

We sailed down the Lynn of Lorn and despite the poor light conditions the narrow entrance to Kerrara Sound became noticeable, due, in no small part, to the frequent

MacBrayne ferries travelling to and from Oban. The ferries point the way in and provided you sail expecting to meet one leaving, they are a great free navigational aid. At 14:13 we were safely tied to a marina pontoon at Ardantive Bay, Kerrara. It had been a pleasant 5½ hour introduction to cruising in the Hebrides and now there was a sheltered berth with a wonderful view of Oban.

*14 June – Day 38. Kerrera Island*

The town of Oban is the gateway to the Hebridean Isles and a constant procession of MacBrayne ferries enter port to collect passengers and supplies bound for the islands of Mull, Colonsay, Coll and Tiree et cetera. The town with its 8,500 people collectively exudes an excited buzz, confident of its place within the economy of Argyll and Bute. What with the bizarre folly of McCaig tower modelled on Rome's Colosseum, the distillery and the railway station, Oban, not unlike Inverness, is an attractive cultural centre of note. Better than the usual boring corporate chain stores, Oban has quirky small shops happy to serve. For yachtsman Oban is also a great place to restock the boat stores or as a crew pick-up point, although a dinghy would be needed to reach the town from the visitor mooring buoys.

Kerrera Island, just ten minutes across the bay from Oban by the marina's courtesy boat, is the more convenient place to leave a yacht for sailors who might prefer a pontoon and regular showers. There is even an outdoor bar and restaurant for those who'd rather dine alfresco close to their boat. It was here that I enjoyed the first of many meals of diver caught Hebridean scallops – in my opinion, the best of seafood on the Scottish coast. The well managed marina is an example of how even the newest published almanac can omit information useful to the yachtsmen. The Kerrera marina was not mentioned in the 2007 Cruising Association almanac, affirming again the importance of gaining local knowledge from fellow sailors met on the cruise. Every opportunity to chat with other yachtsmen should be taken. Ask them where they have been and where they are going. As with the news I had previously gleamed of the recently dredged Scarborough harbour, other yachtsmen can be a vital source of "intelligence". For the record, Kerrera marina can be hailed on VHF radio channel 80. There are some swinging moorings and, of course, many pontoon berths, charged at a rate inclusive of electricity. However, use of the good quality showers cost an additional £1 each and every time. Dare I guess Scottish yachtsmen don't choose to shower quite as often as Sassenachs?

*15 June – Day 39. Kerrera to Tobermory. Passage 26 nm, 5:16 hours*

While Oban was a delight there was a town on a nearby island I felt I should take the chance to visit, although not on the most direct route around the UK. Tobermory on the Isle of Mull has a "must see" reputation.

To reach Tobermory we had to sail northwest, entering the Sound of Mull just to the south of Lismore Island, avoiding the well marked Lady's Rock. The picturesque Castle Duart provided a useful navigational landmark as did the ever present and frequent MacBrayne ferries. Despite the air temperature of just 11 degrees, the passage was glorious and further proof, if proof was needed, that this area is one of the best cruising grounds in the UK.

Tobermory is a pleasant little town and harbour probably in the same premier division as picturesque Salcombe in Devon. The main anchorage was "spotted" with boat moorings and the Highland Development Agency blue visitor buoys with their white tops were a very welcome sight and a great boon for all yacht crews who, like us on Hobo, didn't have power windlasses and ninety or so very heavy metres of calibrated anchor chain. Tobermory harbour did have pontoon berths for about ten yachts yet, at the date of our visit, no toilets or washing facilities close by. So a blue visitor buoy was chosen and my newly acquired hand-me-down Avon inflatable dinghy got its first outing.

*16 June – Day 40. Tobermory*

Happily the local town council has recognised the commercial advantage of beautification – east coast towns should take note of this simple fact – Tobermory is very colourful. Paint is popular and each house, restaurant or pub on the waterfront is gaily painted in a strong colour. The visual effect for arriving yacht crews is almost Mediterranean and consequently very inviting. Also, Tobermory has resisted the political game of re-gaelicisation. The town's name and spelling are both recognisable to English language speakers and, therefore, pronounceable. Perhaps not surprising to rational thinkers, the ease of recognising the name Tobermory has undoubtedly influenced many thousands of travelling yachtsmen to choose to visit the town. Being able to pronounce the name has a valuable commercial advantage. Compare this to those communities now "burdened" by town names imposed to promote the cause of "bonny" celticism. Which would be easier for an English speaking tourist to find? Tobermory or *Tobar Mhoire*. Or what about Oban or *An t-Óban*? The business folk in both towns know the answer to the question. Places with names such as Tigh na bruaich, Rubha Clack-an-Traghaidh, or Gob na Luibe Duibhe just cannot be located using a search engine on the internet. Just how any non-Scot with a road atlas or a navigational chart could direct themselves or others to these sacrifices to linguistic medievalism, I really don't know. But maybe I have missed a key piece to the romantic Celtic puzzle.

Tobermory has a wide selection of restaurants although, disappointingly for us, a number of them claimed to be fully booked on the Friday night we arrived. So popular is Tobermory, it would appear visiting yachtsmen may need to consult their diaries, use mobile phones and call up a couple of days prior to arrival, to secure a table.

The pilot book had informed us that the brightly painted harbour side Mishnish hotel provided showers for visiting dirty sailors. And it did. Yet, whilst without much difficulty a fairly shabby shower room on the first floor of the hotel can be obtained, my experience showed that the one pound coin, required by the machine for the shower, bought just six minutes washing time. This six minutes is sufficient time to adjust the water temperature and apply soap to one's hair – that's all. After six minutes the shower timer clicked off and soap and this wet yachtsman were left in ghastly proximity. Having no additional pound coin with me something similar to a stand up a bed bath was required to recover any remaining dignity. Being public spirited, naturally I wanted to help future yacht crews avoid the unpleasantness I had experienced so I felt a brief complaint to the hotel staff would be reasonable. Surprisingly, I was told by the hotel manager that I was the only person to ever have had difficulty in adjusting the water temperature and showering in just six minutes. It would appear if Scottish sailors shower they shower quickly. So my advice to yachtsmen visiting Tobermory and its Mishnish hotel, always have at least two one pound coins if attempting a shower.

*17 June – Day 41. Tobermory to Craobh Haven. Passage 40 nm, 8:17 hours*

Another early morning start to make the most of the spring

tide, but for our fortitude in shedding sleeping bags so abruptly, we were rewarded by the serene High Definition view of Tobermory reflected in the glassy harbour water. A light breeze did materialise as we entered the Sound of Mull although all too frequently we had to seek added propulsion from the engine. The engine however, continued to cause concern as, when we approached Lady Rock, the diesel bug problem again caused the engine revolutions to drop. Yet more disconnected fuel pipes, filter cleaning and messy system bleeding while Hobo drifted forward, carried by the tide out into the Firth of Lorn. This was hardly what I wanted to experience, or indeed offer my crew, when Hobo was due to enter an area which both the charts and pilot book present to the reader as a worrying obstacle course. A course which is strewn with a selection of whirlpools and tidal races between the islands, but the sun shone and the Hebridean scenery was spectacular.

Our passage navigation called for lots of identification of headlands, islands and rocks but in the calm and strong light conditions, this was amusing rather than alarming – it was a version the child's game "I spy with my little eye something being with R", in our case R was always rock. However, as we sailed down the Sound of Luing trying to pinpoint in the distance the precise gap between the islands Dubh Sgeir and Fladda, it did cause me one or two moments of palpitation. The last of the ebb spring tide eased us past the disturbingly named whirlpool, The Grey Dogs and the equally unpleasantly named island of Scarba. But at this point in the trip I suspected something had gone very wrong with my passage plan calculations as, still 3 nautical miles short of the very crucial tidal gate at Ardluing, I noticed the sudden appearance, around the distant headland, of yachts running before the wind, seemingly blown from the opposite direction. That they have been patiently awaiting a favourable tide to travel north through the narrow Sound was obvious. That these yachts were heading in the opposite direction to Hobo resulted in what for us became a tense hour. I knew from the pilot book that just to west of Ardluing headland lay the infamous Gulf of Corryvreckan, known to be tortured by its dreadful 8 knot current and the legendary boat swallowing whirlpool. This was really a place I didn't want to visit or be swept into. When an authoritative navigational guide warns yachtsmen that Corryvrechan is "very violent and dangerous" and states "no vessel should attempt this passage without local knowledge", a skipper gains more than the odd grey hair or two. An hour can sometimes seem to last an age but I finally managed to slide Hobo around Ardluing headland against the new breeze and tide and then, both crew and skipper suddenly relaxed, the sun felt warm and bird song reached Hobo from the nearby shore. For me, after the occasion of mental chaos, it was all Genesis and I "saw that it was good". We sailed gently northeast past the island of Shuna – this the second island named Shuna since leaving Corpach – to the welcoming although, for me at least, unpronounceable Craobh Haven marina. At 14:57 we secured Hobo to a pontoon finger and were able to rest and enjoy the peace.

Craobh – apparently the word means tree – marina was our home for the night and the nearby Lord of the Isles pub provided a unique, if very dubious, dish of scallops, bizarrely choosing to serve them with onions, gravy and mashed potato – and even more bizarrely, I chose to eat it. I can imagine exactly what Gordon Ramsay would say.

*18 June – Day 42. Craobh Haven to Cairnbaan, Crinan Canal. Passage 13 nm, 8:30 hours*

A yacht bound southwards for the Firth of Clyde has two

choices; to use the Crinan Canal or round the Mull of Kintyre. Importantly, the Crinan allows the less adventurous – or is it the wise yachtsmen – to avoid the long 125 nautical mile sea trek around the Mull of Kintyre to reach the Firth of Clyde. The pilot books and charts for the Kintyre area were hardly encouraging mentioning strong currents, exposed coasts, lack of overnight ports and tidal over falls. Whereas the Crinan canal offers yacht crews the opportunity to bypass all this potential misery. Of course for yachts bound for Ulster the obvious route would be directly to the southwest – repeating the sea passage first the Gaels and then the Scotti took to and from Dalriada and which their descendants were to retrace over so many centuries. Had I not intended to explore the Clyde I would have certainly set off for Ireland from this point. However, given the continued punitive weather, I favoured a sheltered route and therefore chose to use the Crinan Canal.

With an 08:30 start we left the marina in light rain and motored south, down the west side of Ardfern dodging the several well charted rocks that line the coast to Craignish Point. Casting a more than respectful eye over towards the nearby Corryvreckan, I turned Hobo sharp to port into the swirling tidal mixer that is Dorus Mor. Here the very water Hobo sailed on moved at 8 knots. This was definitely a point where I needed the engine to "kick hard" as to get swept out past the island of Garbh Reisa and miss the opening to Loch Crinan would result in, at the very least, an unpleasant six hour detour. However, all went well and the little diesel's pistons thrashed like the spindly legs of a marathon runner sprinting to the finish and we crabbed our way across the current to the Crinan sea lock, arriving at 10:29. The passage from Craobh Haven had been a mere 9 nautical miles taking just over two hours.

Annoyingly for us the lock keeper chose not to answer our

VHF radio call so we picked up a mooring buoy just off the harbour wall to await entry. It was after noon before the lock gate was finally opened and Hobo was raised to the level of freshwater and the small and quite crowded Crinan basin.

After completing the paperwork and obtaining the licence we had a quick cappuccino in the café and then moved off along the narrow canal. First there was a swing bridge, smartly opened for us by the bridge keeper, after a couple of spirited blows on our red plastic horn. This horn blowing exercise was repeated at the Bellanoch Bridge, then came the stair of five locks at Dunardy. It was here we were introduced to the physical challenge of Crinan lock gate operation. On the Caledonian Canal salaried staff operated all the locks, but here on the Crinan, after lock 14, we were required to grab the steel handle ourselves and heave and push the several tons of Victorian timber gate first open and then closed – this four times for each of the five locks. This was different. This was like something devised for a fiendish game show on Japanese TV. Four more locks at Cairnbaan and that was quite enough for the day. At 17:07 Hobo was tied to a pontoon and we looked forward to a well deserved meal at the nearby hotel.

*The Crinan Canal*

For anyone like ourselves who had recently transited the Caledonian Canal, the Crinan is quite a shock. It is so small – a sort of toy-town version of a canal. The Crinan is also very short, cutting just 8 nautical miles across Kintyre to exit on Loch Fyne. The toy-town scale of the canal is unfortunately not matched by the charge levied to use it. At the time of our passage the £86.33 for a nine metre yacht equated to £10.80 per mile. Compare this to the cost of using the Caledonian canal at £2.72 per mile suggests to me the Crinan has been priced to exploit the Clyde-based metropolitan yachtsmen of

Glasgow and Edinburgh. There remains a further sting, as only four out of the fifteen locks on the Crinan are provided with British Waterway staff, eleven locks have to be operated by the yacht crews themselves. We found this process is not easy for anyone weighing under sixteen stone. To move or break free lock gates needs considerable body weight. A lightweight crew or a slim solo sailor would find the Crinan "quite" a physical challenge. I would recommended that a solo sailor or non-rugby playing crew, on entrance to the canal, wait and try to travel in convoy with other craft, thereby allowing a sharing of the workload. Alternatively, the leaflet issued by the Canal's management suggests it is possible, with at least 24 hours notice, to arrange for a "Canal pilot" to accompany short handed vessels although no scale of fees for this service is given.

*19 June – Day 43. Cairnbaan to Tarbert. Passage 14 nm, 7:17 hours*

After one night on the quiet canal the new morning provided rain and the prospect of several more days of unsettled weather. At 08:33 we set off for the nearby Lochgilphead and from there made a visit to the town supermarket. Even with this brief stopover we completed the remaining four locks and were on the sea outside the canal at Ardrishaig Basin by 13:10. Our passage from Cairnbaan had been a mere 4 nautical miles and took 2:15 hours.

For the record our total sea to sea passage time for the Crinan Canal was just 7¼ hours.

Once more on the sea we found we had exchanged the sheltered Inner Hebrides for the glorious Firth of Clyde. At 14:30 we raised the sails and sped southward through Lower Loch Fyne blown before a fresh northeasterly wind. The 10 nautical miles were completed in just two hours and we hurtled into East Loch Tarbert under full sail.

Hobo's arrival was once again verging on brash "attention seeking". As with Eyemouth, I had misinterpreted the scale of the harbour and was, therefore, expecting solid objects to be significantly further apart. Tarbert is surprisingly "cosy". To enter this natural harbour one has slalom to port, and then to starboard, around poles and then avoid a couple of rocks sporting tedious names left by early Gael settlers. Our over hasty and overpowered arrival forced my crew to dance around the coach roof like a Chinese acrobat gathering Dacron and frantically winding coloured sail ties. But once our rig was bound and gagged, Hobo crept in, both skipper and crew trying to look calm and nonchalant before the inevitable audience of watchers.

Tarbert has a long pontoon for visiting yachts and newly built shower block where the gentle female attendant places flowers by the washbasins. By 16:30, over mugs of tea and ginger biscuits, we enjoyed a brief spell of afternoon sunshine that brightly lit the pretty town and sheltered harbour. Tarbert is a truly pleasant place to spend an evening. Unfortunately, overnight the wind blew strongly and more than once I had leave my warm bunk to adjust Hobo's warps and halyards securing things against the wild tempest.

*20 June – Day 44. Tarbert to Rothesay. Passage 23 nm, 5:40 hours*

We spent the morning shopping and I visited a helpful local doctor to get a verdict on a troublesome sore throat – it's not only boats that need occasional maintenance when on a long cruise. At 13:40, after lunch, we set out to sail around the island of Bute intending to reach the bay of Rothesay. From Tarbert we beat across Inchmarnock Water and rounded Ardlamont Point at 16:00. Then north up West Kyle and south down East Kyle. This was truly a Scottish "signature" waterway. Narrow, sheltered and on both sides – green, trees, more green, trees and the occasionally smug looking house. It appears that on the Firth of Clyde waterside homes are a reality – something most of we southerners can only dream of owning in our overpopulated bit of the Union – in Scotland this type of property is not just for the rich Bankers or Stockbrokers of the city. Here almost anyone's dream property can be found on any south facing loch shoreline.

This passage of the Kyles included the interestingly named hamlet of Tigh na Bruaich, apparently an important personal landmark in "coming of age" for my crew Heather and, perhaps almost as tortuous, we then faced the northern "channel" through the Burnt Islands at the northern most point of Bute. Here it was like Hobo had arrived in a scene from movie *The African Queen*, all we needed was a couple of hippos and, like Humphrey Bogart, I would have resorted to swigging neat gin from a bottle. But once safely through the shallows and narrows, a short time later, we arrived in the bay of Rothesay at 19:30. As a fierce downpour looked imminent, rather than investigating the harbour pontoons, we chose to quickly pick up a visitor's mooring for the night off the Bute Sailing Club. And, after some heavy rain, it was a really quiet windless night and in the morning we were rewarded with a very rare event in the summer of 2007 – we took breakfast in the cockpit. Remarkably this was the first time in forty-four days I was able to enjoy breakfast alfresco warmed by the early morning sun.

*21 June – Day 45. Rothesay to Kip via Holy Loch. Passage 22 nm, 7:33 hours*

Bizarre as it may seem, along with the breakfast alfresco, I'll remember the town of Rothesay for the harbour side public toilets. I was amazed to find a tourist group, while on shore leave from a Cruise Ship, visiting the Gentleman's toilets not for the obvious reason but to take photographs of the urinals. That a tour group were guided to a Victorian Gents toilet rather than to any Cathedral or venerable Guildhall building perhaps is an indication of something I am much too discrete to suggest.

Rothesay is also memorable as it helped enrich my understanding of culture north of Hadrian's Wall. Cruising on a yacht can do more than just wet you and cause growth of calluses on your hands, it also provokes thought and, if you have the will, thoughts can prove a catalyst for a wee bit o' study.

It was here I realised that I had encountered several distinct cultures on my cruise around Scotland. On the east coast, I had sensed something of the Picti, that aboriginal group now usually denied a place in populist national history; in the north and the Highlands, the Caledonii, another aboriginal people noted by the Romans and now at least commemorated on postcards and souvenirs; on the west coast and the Hebrides I had seen the signage in celebration of the Gaels who arrived here from the island we now refer to as Ireland. However, I also frequently mentally noted throwaway references to another ethnic group inhabiting pre-second millennium Scotia. It appears there were other people adding their culture and genes to the haggis pudding that is history – the Norse. While today's Scottish nationalists sidestep the Picti preferring to emphasise each and every aspect of "Highland" imagery, the Norse – call them Viking if you like – are also marginalised. However, the truth is the Norse undoubtedly settled the northern and western islands and surrounding coast from the middle to late first millennium. So fundamental was Norse settlement that documents even record a treaty in 1098 between a Scottish King called Edgar and Magnus

III, King of Norway where the former recognised Norse sovereignty over the peoples and land in the west. Here on Rothesay, I again felt the need to question the validity of so many Gael place names and the Celtic "heritage" industry. Rothesay is a Norse name and it originally referred not to the town but to the whole island of Bute. Surely if Anglo-Scottish place names are to continue to be replaced by Gaelic on charts and street signs, the old Norse names should also be added?

As I continued to explore the Firth of Clyde I would later sense another cultural group. In the south – the Scottish lowlands around Troon – dare I mention the Anglo-Saxons? The people of today's Scotland are definitely far greater than the sum of political slogans.

At 10:30, after the shopping trip in Rothesay, we let go the mooring and pointed Hobo eastwards into the Firth of Clyde. The sun shone and the calm sheltered waters re-confirmed my opinion that the Inner Hebrides and the Firth of Clyde offer the best cruising grounds for yachtsmen in the UK. However, we alone appeared to be enjoying the scenery. Unlike any day spent sailing on the Solent, here there were only two other yachts and the ever present MacBayne ferries to avoid. We had the Firth to ourselves. While our destination was the nearby Kip marina, the day was so pleasant we decided to explore more of the Clyde and visit Holy Loch. From Skelmorlie Point to Holy Loch it was a mere 7 nautical miles, and just past the attractive looking town of Dunoon.

Holy Loch is less than a mile wide at its broadest part and two miles long at high water. Regrettably for us visitors, the story of how it gained the name "holy" seems to have been lost – someone needs to find it.

The reason the Loch's name sparked mental recognition in this fifty-year-old male was due to the United States naval base which, for 31 years from 1960, dominated the scenery and local culture. This was, dare I suggest, a form of imperial occupation by nuclear powered and armed warships and submarines of a foreign nation. Ironically, the final liberation of Scotland's Holy Loch was not due to democratic action within local nationalists or the UK parliament but the actions of the brave Soviet people. The collapse of the Communist led Soviet Union finally brought peace to Holy Loch. Today the Loch is tranquillity personified and its marina now a sheltered base of native mariners rather than Uncle Sam's gun toting, floating "defenders".

The delights of Holy Loch were quickly experienced and we sailed off to Kip, a 620 berth, well managed marina that was easily located by a huge and now redundant chimney and the tumble of concrete blocks that make the pair of breakwaters.

*22 – 23 June. Days 46 – 47. Kip*

Although the nearby village of Inverkip had a rail link into Glasgow, I felt a "jobs day" was needed and a mixture of repairs, cleaning and laundry filled the hours. On the next day, crew Heather had arranged a "bus man's holiday". After 47 days on board Hobo I became guest on another yacht. The imminent departure of my crew of the last fourteen days had created an opportunity to meet two local sailors who together owned a Moody 346 yacht. Stewart and Cathy kindly invited us to spend the day with them and despite the steady drizzle, we set sail in the Moody for Loch Goil 12 miles from Kip.

Stretching due north from Kip, there is Loch Long which led this unsuspecting sailor into the murky world of the Cold War, spying and vast military spending. For on the east side of Loch Long there is a floating facility to do, well, something unmentionable to the UK's nuclear submarine fleet. A huge grey floating shed threatens the Loch side and the police boats, cameras and masses of barbed wire confirm, for the innocent, this building is definitely not friendly. Looking like something from a James Bond movie, the building has turrets on all four corners and on the land side, a double wire fence that marches aggressively up the hillside. This could be some type of nightmare fantasy for agent 007 or his enemy Spectre but no, this is Coulport, Scotland and its nearby associated Faslane base.

Further north and off to the west from Long Loch was our destination Loch Goil and as we motored slowly up the scenic valley we passed yet more of the secret world of Britain's Weapons of Mass Destruction. Here was another Naval facility with its submarine now about to depart to the dark beyond. Nervously, we crept past under threatening gaze of the military police with their even more threatening machine guns.

Subsequently, and in total contrast to what we had passed earlier, at the head of the loch we enjoyed a barbecue and a few pleasant hours before the return trip to Kip. Just as a postscript to things military, it is probably not comforting for the nearby population of Glasgow to know that had there ever been a nuclear war, Glasgow and the nearby lochs of the Clyde would have been the target for more than a reasonable share of the world's atomic stockpile. My guess is that, rather than defending Scotland from possible attack, the existence of nuclear naval bases outside Glasgow would have brought about its total annihilation.

*24 June – Day 48. Kip to Troon. Passage 27 nm, 5:45 hours*

After crew Heather's departure, I became a solo sailor once more, and it was with mixed emotions I set out on the passage to Troon. After the reassurance of sharing the potential trials of the unknown with another person, it was now again all up to me and me alone. Solo sailing is more a profound personal test of emotional character rather than of sailing prowess.

The weather forecast suggested a fine morning but with the possibility of strong offshore winds later. However, I anticipated I could reach Troon by early afternoon and Troon was important to me as it was close to Prestwick airport, the arrival point of my next plucky crew member.

At 08:34 I left Kip and headed due south towards Largs and the island of Great Cumbrae. By 10:00 I was abeam the church spires of Largs town, quite picturesque and an easy passage via the sheltered channel. As Hobo sailed a beam reach out once more into the Firth of Clyde, the freshening north wind reminded me of the earlier forecast. But it was just 12 nautical miles from Portencross to Troon and, happily, there was still some hazy sunshine.

At 13:30 the wind dropped and I noticed a dark line of cloud building from the east. I anticipated a little "trouble" so reduced sail by tucking the first of my three slab reefs into the main. Within just 10 minutes the new wind arrived, increased and a vicious squall forced the second reef. As Hobo bounded across Irvine Bay, I attempted to identify the entrance to Troon harbour. As always, the grey of the shore line matched exactly the grey of the breakwater piers. In a century where even office cleaners permanently wear "hi-visibility" clothing to ensure anyone is able to locate them in an "emergency dirt situation", it is more than frustrating that harbour masters around Britain don't similarly adorn harbour entrances with florescent plastic boards. However, though the gloom, I fixed my eyes on a small gap in the grey and at 14:00 Hobo arrived in Troon outer harbour. From here, once over a shallow 2.6 metre sill, I motored into the 400 berth Troon Yacht Haven. For once the weather forecast had been "spot on" and I tied to a pontoon finger in driving rain and violent northeast wind.

*25 June – Day 49. Troon*

Here the very topography of the region had changed from that of north Scotland. Gone were the "signature" hills, glens and lochs. Here around Troon the lowlands looked and felt very like, dare I suggest, like northern England.

Troon has two major advantages for the cruising yachtsman. Firstly, it is just 6 miles from Prestwick airport with its international air connections. Secondly, anyone with an addiction to that wonderful Scottish game Golf would probably delight in being so close to the greens of Royal Troon.

The wind blew hard all day and the radio news reports told me of more low pressure weather systems dumping massive rainfall in England. There had been floods and deaths. While for me, after 49 days on the boat, the stories seemed to be about far away places I once knew, the subject of mutant summer weather was all too personal.

So I busied myself with all the little boaty type jobs that, for sailors, are a constant preoccupation. And there was more food shopping in expectation of the later arrival of my new crew member Anders, a 6½ foot tall Swede. I had sailed several times before with Anders on his very beautiful and very Swedish long, low and thin yacht on the Baltic. Around the coast of Sweden sailing and sailors are encouraged and yachting is very much a family activity. It would be Anders' first experience of coping with our big tides and the ambivalent nature of our town councils to visiting sailors. His flight from Stockholm arrived at Prestwick just before midnight, and soon after this I heard his knock on the hull, confirming just how convenient Troon harbour is for the airport.

*26 June – Day 50. Troon to Stranraer. Passage 44 nm, 7:00 hours*

The weather forecast was for squally north by northwest winds of force 5 to 6. The outlook for the next few days was similar so there was little advantage in awaiting a more gentle introduction to UK sailing. The natural shelter of Firth of Clyde would ensure the sea state remained reasonable and the entrance to our intended destination of Loch Ryan was broad although open to the wind direction. As I didn't want Anders to have to spend his first few days captive on shore in Troon, my decision was to push westwards and hope the weather proved better than the forecast.

At 09:30 we left Troon harbour and under full main and jib, beam reached off at 6.4 knots in bright sunshine but a cold north wind. Being in the lee of the Isle of Arran meant the sea state was slight so we had an exhilarating sail along the coast past Ayr, but once the firth opened out, a moderate swell started to create the corkscrew motion seldom popular with we mortals. With Hobo "galloping" across the waves, preparation and eating of our lunch time "Cornish" pasties was a little stressed. The first reef was required as the wind increased and the boulder shaped isle of Ailsa Craig lay still ahead on the starboard bow. Anders was having the proverbial "baptism of fire" and he pointedly kept bringing to my attention all the small harbours as we passed by. That these small harbours were open to the northerly swell, and therefore unavailable to Hobo, merely added tension to the cockpit atmosphere. The wind was rising and, yes, we were sailing in fresh conditions along what was an unwelcoming lee shore. Neither of us had sailed these waters and I was relying on the chart and almanac for information about Loch Ryan still three or more hours away. Naturally, I tried to seem confident about what lay ahead. Of course, doubt did play on my mind and I checked and re-checked my passage plan.

While perfectly safe in the conditions, the rapid motion of the boat was becoming uncomfortable. I didn't want to sail more water than necessary and there was the suggestion that there might be rough seas off Mulleur Point, just west of the entrance to Loch Ryan, so the usual routine search of the horizon took place. Happily, just when we needed it, the precise whereabouts of entrance to the loch was revealed by arrival of car ferries from Northern Ireland. With this confirmation of the GPS chart plotter we hurtled on and yes, we did find the sea worsened as we approached the mouth of the loch.

As we bore off away from the wind on to a run and pointed Hobo's bow straight down the loch, unfortunately, we saw the spectre of a huge white floating car park approaching from the opposite direction. The sheer size and speed of "fast cat" ferries can only really be appreciated when on the deck of a small yacht. As we tried to decide the best course to steer to stay away from this roaring sea monster, it turned and turned again following the dredged channel.

Rather like two car drivers in an American fifties teen movie, we shot towards each other. Hobo surfing the waves at 9 knots and the Seacat piercing the same waves from the other direction at more than 40. This was sort of a game of marine chicken. Who would veer off first. Happily the Captain of this aqua starship was skilled and respectful of the limited speed of a thirty foot sailing yacht. The fast cat gave us ample sea room and we escaped the worst of its turbulent wash. However, the moment when I looked through the Seacat – that is under the car deck and between the tall twin hulls to the land and trees beyond – a cold cold chill ran through me. It was like looking down the throat of a voracious monster and seeing the other side – the inside. Perhaps modern navigational charts should reuse the famous old legend 'here be monsters'.

In this situation one quickly realises that, despite well meaning Marine and Coastguard Agency guidelines, yachtsmen are powerless to avoid fast cat ferries travelling at 40 knots. By the time you see them, you are already too close for comfort. A yacht travelling at, say, 5 knots can do very little if, unfortunately, it finds itself in the path of a fast cat and can only rely on the Ferry's helmsman taking avoiding action. Staring straight down the throat of this star trek type sea craft one feels very very small. However, in our case, this beast of Stranraer, called HSS Voyager, roared by Hobo and we steered on into the long 7 mile bottle that is Loch Ryan.

We had overcome the first obstacle but a second soon materialised. Loch Ryan is shallow and for Anders, my Swedish crew, more used to sailing in the rock strewn but deep Baltic, shallow water is something quite frightening. Even in the main shipping channel the water appeared to be no more than 5 metres deep. Ahead of us lay several buoys and to starboard, the long sand spit behind which, according to the pilot book, there was a sheltered anchorage known as the Wig. I should have known nothing substantial could be named Wig. While perhaps this might be a comfortable spot for the night during any normal summer, I felt we needed something a little more rooted to the earth. From our moving vantage point the Wig looked very threadbare and hardly any covering of note. There were no other yachts, moorings, or other signs that the Wig was a popular shelter. So the Wig was "off" and, therefore, the main harbour of Stranraer was now our only alternative.

Several requests to the Stranraer harbour master made over the VHF radio produced nil response. However, suddenly a voice from a fishing boat named Orca responded to our call and this Orca turned out to be an angling boat owned and run by the said missing harbour master. As luck would have it, he was following us closely down the loch. Having received the harbour master's assurance that Stranraer would be able to offer Hobo a safe haven for the night, we continued on course, blown down the narrow channel to the far dead end that is Stranraer.

Once through the narrow entrance of the harbour we tied Hobo alongside a very comfortable looking Moody Eclipse. Our average speed over the seven hours was 6.5 knots and Anders and I were both more than happy to rest. Unfortunately, the tidal harbour allowed the swell from the north to curl through breakwaters so Hobo rocked and rolled the night away. The evening's R&R ashore offered little to the hungry crew that wasn't a fish n' chip and burger café.

*27 – 28 June. Days 51 – 52. Stranraer*

Fifty-one days aboard and still the British summer refused to treat we islanders with respect or kindness. My routine varied a little bit but everything revolved around the weather forecast. Here in Stranraer, seemingly trapped at the bottom of a 7 mile long "bottle" open to the northwest wind, the strong force 6 continued to blow directly into the loch making an escape attempt futile.

In the morning, although thankfully a near peaceful night had passed, the wind re-awoke and again drove an annoying choppy sea into the harbour. Hobo and the comfortable Moody we are lying alongside, bounced about in a jolting dance that lasted until two o'clock in the afternoon – warps straining, fenders fending and me trying not to worry about Hobo's safety. I feared tomorrow morning with a high tide we might again experience the rock 'n' roll torment.

Ah, wonderful Stranraer. Yet another day in which

to enjoy our now regular cafe and a breakfast bacon roll, although, for reasons beyond me Swedish crew, Anders, had difficulty understanding the concept and phrase "bacon roll". I tried to understand his question – to me a bacon roll is a bacon roll – but admit it was beyond me. Perhaps philosopher Jean-Paul Sartre also had the problem of bacon rolls in mind when his own existentialist questioning tortured his acolytes. But after breakfast it was to the town library for Internet browsing – we were both by now members. Here we joined the zombies of unemployed, apparently habitual Internet users, created to occupy IT rooms in libraries all across the UK. Then next it was off to the Stranraer leisure centre, not for a swim or to use the gym but, like other tramps, for a hot shower. It is comforting to have routines and in Stranraer we needed comfort. I hoped maybe we would be able to escape tomorrow. But on this day in late June everything and everyone was damp. Fortunately, at least, there were none of the infamous Scottish midges – perhaps they all drowned.

*29 June – Day 53. Stranraer to Bangor NI. Passage 39 nm, 7:45 hours*

While the weather forecast was still less than comforting, Anders and I both felt a strong need to move on, so at the very serious time of 04:30 we headed Hobo out into the loch and navigated the narrow channel northwards towards our "freedom". Of course day break was also the time for the Seacat to make its rush for Northern Ireland and soon one prowled up from astern, at the same time both threatening and exciting, as we again witnessed the power of this towering sea monster. The fresh northerly wind was blowing on the nose, so the little engine "puffed" its best, and we took two hours to round the headland and turn on to the compass course for Ireland. Unfortunately, before seeing Ireland we saw – and felt – a rough confused sea as the swell bounced back off Corsewall Point and the tidal current "kicked" against yet another land mass. Still with two reefs in the mainsail and the working jib set, we were on a close reach and both Hobo and the spray flew. Having Ireland in sight, while, at the same time, carefully noting the procession of dark squalls bearing down from the North Channel, we were kept very busy. Hobo was happy and a happy boat should be enough for any skipper and crew. As usual, I advised the coast guard of our intended passage and we rocked and rolled our way across to Ireland just as countless generations of travellers had done before.

By 08:00 we were beyond the halfway point and, as usual, this fact changed the emotional focus, from "can we really get across?" to "where exactly is it"? Belfast Lough was our destination, although shallow and occasionally rough, it is a reassuringly broad target, with the unpleasantly named Blackhead light as a navigational mark. The Lough also provided harbours at Carrickfergus on the north shore and Bangor on the south, so we were happy to have options suited to wind from all points of the compass. Since Bangor allowed Hobo a course "freer" from the fresh northerly breeze, we steered towards what we hoped might be a late Ulster fry breakfast.

However, our arrival at Bangor was not without confusion. While the Lough – and early in this tale when writing of the Caledonian Canal I did warn the reader that after the locks, and lochs would come this loughs – was easily identified quite soon after leaving the Galloway coast, the precise location of Bangor on the Lough's south shore was more difficult. All too often, from a visual point low on the sea, the coast appears grey and featureless. At 5 miles out, Bangor remained a place of mystery and, despite the confidence of the chart plotter, I remained in doubt of its location until the harbour breakwater at last became visible.

At 11:17, after many tiring trips up and down the companion way steps to consult the chart table, we downed sails and made for the entrance of Bangor marina to have Hobo safely berthed and skipper and crew off for a hot shower at 11:45.

It is perhaps worth confessing here that, prior to this cruise, I had always thought Bangor was in North Wales and, due to the illusion created by a remembered hit record from the late 1970s, the occasional holiday destination of 19th-century mill workers:

Didn't we have a lovely time
The day we went to Bangor
A beautiful day, we had lunch on the way
And all for under a pound, you know
That on the way back I cuddled with Jack
And we opened a bottle of cider
Singing a few of our favourite songs
As the wheels went around

Debbie Cook

But once safely ashore in Northern Ireland I learned there were indeed two towns by the name of Bangor. After a visit to the 21st-century boon to all itinerant sailors, the local library with its public Internet access, I learned that Bangor in Ulster is an ancient settlement, its name derived from an Irish language word 'Beanncher' meaning fenced enclosure. However, what to me seemed bizarre, in North Wales, almost directly opposite its namesake across the Irish Sea, the other town of Bangor embraces the same meaning but claims the name was derived from the Welsh language. Oh, how the hoards of little nationalists of this once United Kingdom now struggle to create "cosy" myths to support their preferred separate antiquity. So Bangor, Welsh or Irish? The truth, as a TV sci-fi series once proclaimed, "is out there".

*30 June – 1 July. Days 54 – 55. Bangor NI*

Another day and another low pressure weather system – and two more reported to be tracking their way in. Published statistics started to prove what any sailor on a fifty-five day sojourn already knew, summer 2007 was dreadful. The newspaper headlines declared 'The wettest June on a record'. Of course these media "sound-bites" are suspect, but there certainly had been a lot rain and, since I started in early May, Hobo had been assailed by low pressures and frustrating winds that had not mirrored the orthodox summer norm. Westerly wind had been as rare as an honest politician.

So another day in port as the Hobo collective, that is my crew and I, debated the forecast and the prospect for a better wind direction. We decided to wait in the hope tomorrow we would have a westerly wind. To improve conditions in our small living space we turned the boat around in the marina berth, stopping the rain from driving into the companionway and cabin. The hum of the little electric fan heater competed with the pitter patter of the Ulster rain.

Bangor, Northern Ireland became our continued haven and Bangor is a fun town. The mark of Victorian taste is still present and both character and community benefit from this. The marina is large and well run and, if one has to be harbour-bound, Bangor is not a disappointment. I liked Ulster folk. They smiled and readily exuded uncomplicated warmth without guile. While closely related by genes to their brethren in western Scotland, Ulster folk seemed to lack the latter's dour, sometimes gloomy and prickly countenance. After three weeks cruising Scotland, the simple Ulster humour, so freely offered, was refreshing.

Perhaps a cliché observation but it was hard for me not to feel a little like Odysseus – battling to reach home. Since turning south, my focus had been to get Hobo back to Greenwich – not because Greenwich was particularly homely but because Greenwich represented "peace" and completion. I hungered for the deep satisfaction of reaching home but, like Odysseus, each time I thought I'd overcome an obstacle, another one appeared. Days passed and a homeward warm wind and smooth sea were always just perhaps another day ahead. The continuous news reports on the radio suggested there was indeed another larger world outside my odyssey but for me it was only my voyage that occupied my thoughts and body. I am Odysseus – but without the Penelope thing.

A small boat with a crew in gloomy wet weather is more tense than a small boat solo. There is something strangely oppressive in having to share confinement and disappointment. If I were in prison I think I'd prefer a solitary cell.

The continued dire weather led me to repeatedly rework and rework the various route options for getting Hobo further south. However, the Welsh coast option of Cardigan Bay to me still looked unwelcoming to a yacht with a 1.7 metre deep fin keel. Here on the Irish side, the coast looked better, although not if faced with southeasterly winds. I poured over the charts again and again looking for inspiration for another route but, of course, none arrived. There are only those two options available to make passage south and I'd chosen Ireland so I had to be patient and draw on the philosophy of all sage mariners. Await a favourable wind – don't rush – accept the weather for what it is, an elemental condition greater and more significant than man. The weather, however unsympathetic to my personal voyage, is green, natural and free. The forces and actions of man are not.

The difference between my personal odyssey and a larger outside world full of politics and convention was put into marked contrast on Saturday. Somebody tried to attack the people of my home town of London with two car bombs. Happily they didn't succeed. Awaiting favourable weather in Bangor perhaps didn't seem so bad an option.

The radio forecasted a southeasterly wind up to force 7 so it seemed a good idea to visit to the local tourist office for recreation ideas. Anders chose a visit to Belfast but, as I knew this city well and didn't relish the train journey, I remained in Bangor. I discovered the 30th of June had been chosen by the town council of Groomsport for their annual Eagle Wing festival. As Groomstown was just east of Bangor along Belfast Lough and as I needed amusement, I thought I would take a trip to experience a little local Ulster culture. However, when I arrived I soon learned that this festival is an example of bizarre cultural confusion and a product of an "educated" island people's desire to create myths far removed from any rational interpretation of history.

In a small harbour side fisherman's cottage I was to learn that the Eagle Wing was a sailing ship of 150 tons, which in November of the year 1636 set out from Groomsport with 140 Protestant fundamentalists bound for New England. The story offered to the audience of tourists was of how these Protestant people had suffered religious persecution in Protestant Ulster and therefore sought "freedom" in a New World. Their quest was portrayed as a heroic and wholesome.

Of course a person of today, regrettably used to considering religious fundamentalism such as that manifested on the streets of London, might perhaps interpret the story differently. I might suggest that, in truth, the story of Eagle

Wing is not one of heroic success, but of foolish failure. After eight weeks struggling with the weather in the Atlantic ocean, the religious "guides" aboard the ship decided God didn't want them to reach the New World and the ship turned back. Naturally the Groomsport storytellers made no mention of what happened to the 140 hungry and well salted fundamentalists when they returned penniless to Ulster.

More than just this bizarre celebration of religious intolerance and failure, what really confused me was, rather than a celebration of seventeen-century Ulster culture, the Eagle Wing festival at Groomsport drew exclusively on American western imagery lifted from Hollywood movies. At Groomsport, on the sizable outdoor music stage a country and western band played Johnny Cash favourites. Walking around the stalls, I saw very dubious looking American Indian squaws accompanied by equally questionable Indian warriors. Even the harbour side Cunningham coffee shop boasted an American menu served by pretty waitresses wearing cowboy hats, boots and jeans.

It was beyond my understanding just why the local community organisers, each year choose to link together a seventeenth-century ship carrying Ulster Scot Protestant malcontents, ironically failing to reach a place known as New England, with the fake imagery of nineteenth-century American cowboys and Indians. "Family fun" perhaps but disappointingly misleading and hollow. Happily for me the apple and cinnamon hot scones served in Cunningham's coffee shop were superb.

On Sunday the legacy of Tony Blair's wars arrived north, just across the water in Scotland. Glasgow airport was the scene of a despicable terror attack when two males tried to blow up a passenger terminal. Anders, perhaps thinking of his flight home, looked a little concerned.

*2 July – Day 56. Bangor NI to Ardglass NI. Passage 36 nm, 6:21 hours*

We were up early and at 06:00 made a start to catch the tide and best use the small "weather window" suggested by the latest forecast. Out into the Lough and eastwards past Groomsport and by 06:30 onto Dunaghadee Sound where we closely adhered to the passage advice given by the almanac.

The south-going tide runs strongly between Copeland Island, Deputy Reef and the coast, so we were careful to identify each buoy marking the safe route. As we swept by Copelands Marina at Donaghadee, we noted its rocky entrance, and I for one shuddered as I imagined attempting to enter in a fresh southeasterly wind.

As we approached South Rock we had a few stressful minutes when the light house indicated by the chart seemed to have multiplied in real life. Marking a rocky shoal, the exact position is, of course, reasonably important to mariners. The confusion onboard Hobo was finally dispelled when we deduced that, although the chart clearly revealed one light house, the old, now redundant structure remained on a solitary rock some distance inshore from its successor. A rapid change of course was required.

We made good progress and at 09.50 we were able to look eastwards and consider making for the entrance of Strangford Lough with the marina at the strangely named Portaferry, a potential overnight haven. While a true cruising yacht would probably have chosen this picturesque sheltered inlet, passage makers such as we on Hobo had to consider the possibility of our next exit. The almanac contained words that were enough to deter our entry, 'Up to 7 knots current' and on the ebb, 'dangerous breaking seas in fresh winds from the southwest to east'. Given the continued disturbed weather systems, a southeasterly wind was likely and we didn't want to be marooned in Strangford Lough. Of course with hindsight, four days in Strangford, harbour bound, would have offered far more pleasure than the same time at Ardglass, but we were ruled by the immediate needs of our onward passage to Dublin Bay.

At 11:58 we approached Ardglass harbour and found, as so often before, once past the breakwater, the haven was revealed to be much smaller than imagined. There were fishing boats moored to port, separated by a small rocky outcrop from the tiny, but friendly Phennick Cove marina to starboard. At 12:11 we moored on a pontoon and made ready to discover the "delights" of a small fishing village.

*3 – 6 July. Days 57 – 60. Ardglass NI*

Ardglass, Northern Ireland is a small town. It's on the possible list, yet to be written, of places I'd never heard of and never expected to visit. A more normal tourist would probably not choose to head their car down the road leading to this fishing harbour which first appeared on the written record in 1178 when property investor and Norman warlord John de Courcey decided to add the local real estate to his portfolio. However, when one is cruising, the wind, and the need to find staging posts between the more major ports, means small, sleepy towns emerge onto the passage plan. Ardglass proved to be a town so sleepy that, even in July, the pubs here had shutters closed during the day, and none of them appeared to serve food.

The town's only other entry into wider known popular history was due to Belfast born singer/songwriter Van Morrison. He sang about once stopping here for food, but quite how he found any retailer open was to remain a mystery to us and I, for one, would have loved to dine on Mussels or indeed a coney casserole:

On and on, over the hill to Ardglass
In the jamjar, autumn sunshine, magnificent
And all shining through

Stop off at Ardglass for a couple of jars of
Mussels and some potted herrings in case
We get famished before dinner

On and on, over the hill and the craic is good
Heading towards Coney Island

But Ardglass has a good harbour and it does have, when you can find them, friendly people. It all felt a little bizarre though. As we walked the town after another Hobo lunch, it was as if we had stumbled on a forgotten set for an EU subsidised spaghetti western. Silent houses, closed shops and no-one on the streets. This apparent lack of commerce and people added to a ghostly sound that echoed around the empty town. It evoked memories of that scene from the movie *An American Werewolf in London* – the one where the two lone travellers arrive at the pub called the Slaughtered Lamb. But happily for us this howling sound was not coming from supernatural beings. Far from it, in fact, in Ardglass you can see wild life adopting human habits. Nine seals appear to have taken up residency in the harbour and have taught themselves how to "stand" together in a group on a submerged rock, leaving just their heads above the water. Each high tide, like a group of the long-term unemployed standing outside a council estate betting shop, these seals get together and howl a melancholy "song". Nine blackheads a howling. Somehow less than cute and more than a bit unsettling.

Another day passed and the Met Office atmospheric pressure

chart showed four lows rotating around and over the United Kingdom. "Slow-moving", the radio stated. Yes – right, I'd lost count of how many days my passage plan had been disrupted by gangs of slow moving anti-social low pressures.

Sailing solo does, at least, have one significant benefit – when solo there is no need to feel guilty about weather delays. When you have a crew who has travelled many miles specifically to sail, and the wind blows from the wrong direction, and the rain patters on the deck, being port bound means a skipper feels responsible. There is an unspoken requirement on a sailing skipper to provide sailing. Being cabin and harbour bound when sailing solo is very frustrating, and sometimes even depressing, but when there is crew, there emerges a deeply unpleasant feeling for the skipper which I might describe as guilt. It is perhaps this guilt that sometimes leads otherwise experienced skippers to make foolish decisions, choosing to head their yachts out into an expected storm or a dark threatening night.

Awaiting a favourable wind, Anders and I wandered the streets wearing our only clothes waterproof enough for the weather, namely our sailing jackets, bright enough to cause a migraine for any local inhabitants – had we met any. But stuck as we were, all roads from Ardglass seemed to lead to Downpatrick, the major town of County Down. So a bus trip past the cottages known as Coney Island and a few hours in Downpatrick there to see the Cathedral, and my opportunity to pay respects at, what is reputed to be the grave of the only Briton the Irish people appear prepared to embrace as kindred, St Patrick. The legend is that the patron Saint of Ireland was buried here around the year 461, retiring after ridding Ireland of snakes and leaving as his legacy, the Catholic Church. In retrospect, after so many years of sectarian "troubles", some people might possibly claim it was not such a good swap.

After playing the enforced tourist in County Down for three days, my Swedish crew, Anders, left. I stayed. Anders who was more used to warm glorious Baltic summers and long days sailing a sheltered tide free sea, decided to salvage some of his annual leave and return to the land of blondes, Ikea and Volvos. The logistics were not simple. The local bus went to Downpatrick and from there a second bus took him into the Irish Republic and on to Dublin airport. I did feel guilty that, after nine days in the non-summer of 2007, together we only managed three days at sea. Frustrating for me but probably far worse for Anders.

The weather forecast for the preceding four days had constantly warned that a cauldron of lows circulating the UK would deliver a gale. We had waited and waited and, of course, the actual wind reaching Ardglass had been relatively docile. This quite naturally increased my feelings of frustration – knowing we could have left and could have made the next port on the passage plan. However, on July 5$^{th}$, the weather forecast demanded respect. The morning started with a light westerly then the wind backed to south then southeast and rose to force 6. The coastguard repeated their earlier warning of an imminent gale – although from the west. The weather was at last ugly and I stayed below deck, Hobo, on her pontoon was buffeted by wind and rain and rough harbour water. Proof, if proof were necessary, that even though they're unreliable, the weather forecasts cannot safely be ignored.

Foolishly I asked myself again "Will I ever get out of Ardglass?" A high pressure system the weather forecasters implied might arrive by the weekend, had seemingly mutated demonically into yet another low.

*7 July – Day 61. Ardglass NI to Dun Laoghaire IRE. Passage 63 nm, 12:38 hours*

After the storm the next dawn arrived cold and grey, but

reassuringly gentle, so I rushed to escape harbour and push south. It was hardly the best start for an Englishman, as my breakfast tea had to be postponed due to the bottled gas for the cabin stove failing to burn. The evening before I'd changed the gas bottle for the new one, bought from a chandler back at Inverness. Whatever it was filled with, it wouldn't burn on Hobo's stove, so I hurriedly changed back to the old nearly empty bottle. So it was a slightly agitated solo sailor who started the engine at 05:35 and rushed to leave Ardglass harbour. What lay ahead was to be the longest solo passage so far and this fact, combined with too many days spent waiting for a "weather window", meant I was nervous. Too much preparation and reading had cluttered my mind with "monsters" and dangers. I knew I had to just get out there and "get back on the horse".

My plan was to steer south, southeast, butting the last two hours of the north going tidal stream, and then turn due south when off the entrance to Carlingford Lough. There was a fresh breeze from the northeast and Hobo was soon bouncing over the waves at a velocity that resulted in the apparent wind, created by the boat speed, moving forward close on the bow. Consequently lots of spray and a heeling boat dictated first one reef and then the second. At 07:00 the frisky conditions provoked the autohelm to have a "nervous breakdown", leaving me little choice but to switch it off and manually take the tiller. Happily the skill of the designer of the Hanse 301 had created a well balanced hull and, with a little care, I was able to trim the sheets and succeeded in getting Hobo to steer herself for short periods. So if anyone repeats to you the old myth of fin and spade hull configurations being no good for cruising – they're wrong. So within two hours of leaving Ardglass, I was without an autohelm and therefore I faced the reality that, for the next ten hours I would steer and, at the same time, navigate, reef sails, remove reefs (repeat several times) feed myself et cetera.

The Mountains of Mourne provided both a dramatic backdrop to the white caped waves and boosted the vicious off shore winds that whooshed Hobo forward towards the Irish Republic. At 09:29 Hobo was 11 nautical miles off Ballagan Point and, for the first and only time on my around UK cruise, I hoisted a national courtesy flag.

By 13:00, then east of the Skerries, Hobo had averaged a speed of 6.2 knots since leaving Ardglass. From this point the west wind eased and became more variable. Sun and squalls took it in turns to first burn and then soak me and I guessed I would arrive looking not unlike the Ancient Mariner in the poem by Samuel Coleridge.

With the coast of the Irish Republic an indistinct and long way to starboard, the island of Lamby and headland off Howth were in the distance, constituting my next land marks. It was hard work and what seemed a very long time until I was able to round the headland into Dublin Bay but, once there, I was greeted by the signs of "fellowship" – other yachts. Despite being a Monday, Dublin Bay was criss-crossed by a variety of craft, all enjoying the late afternoon breeze and sunshine. This was a welcome sight and for an hour or two I allowed myself to believe that perhaps at last, summer had arrived.

Dun Laoghaire harbour lay on the south side of the bay and the impressive Victorian breakwaters opened, "Russian Doll" like, to reveal more breakwaters within. Happily for a very tired sailor, by 17:09 Hobo was safely alongside the visitors pontoon T, which, I was later to learn, was far enough away from the marina office to need its own postal code. I had arrived very relieved, excited and more than a little salt encrusted.

*8 – 9 July. Days 62 – 63. Dun Laoghaire IRE*

Not having sailed on the Irish coast before, when I read on the chart the name of the largest marina in Ireland at Dun Laoghaire, quite naturally I believed I was sailing to somewhere called "dun la-og-haire". In this innocence, I believe quite reasonably, when I finally approached Dublin Bay, I made repeated calls via the VHF radio to the "dun la-og-haire" marina requesting a berth and advice. I was disappointed not to get any response. With hindsight obviously the marina office staff could hear my call but they chose not to recognise my words. In this, I was a victim of the curse of "Gaelic" cultural absolutists, who insist on refusing to recognise spelling or pronunciation of Irish names in English, the second most understood language in the world.

Once Hobo was berthed and I visited the marina office to pay the overnight charge, I was surprised to learn that the name of the town and marina was universally referred to as "Dun Leary". A little research at the library provided the answer to this confusion. Dun Leary was the spelling used by most, if not all, literate Irish people until 1821 when the British government foolishly renamed the place Kingstown – perhaps in recognition of the then huge civil engineering project to build the breakwaters creating a naval harbour. This unnecessary symbol of Imperialism was removed in 1921, however, then the leaders of the new Irish Free State chose to burden the town with an equally unnecessary and foolish piece of gesture politics by insisting the town's name be spelt in Gaelic. From then onwards million and millions of visitors to Ireland have been embarrassed and confused when asking directions or referring to the town's name.

Let's be honest and call a spade a spade. Insisting on writing Dun Laoghaire in replacement of Dun Leary is, in my opinion, as silly as it would be for the English to vandalise the name London back to its first millennium equivalent “Londinium” or insist everyone use the name of its fabled “Celtic” predecessor, *Kaerlundein.*

Dun Laoghaire, whilst a large modern town just outside the city of Dublin, seemed to me to have a frustrating habit of closing just when sailors needed it to be open. On Saturday evening and Sunday morning shops in Dun Laoghaire were shuttered and very closed for business – peculiar for a town with an international ferry link and a major yachting centre.

With another new morning the weather forecasts, which had previously promised fairish westerly winds and a smooth passage onward to Milford Haven – perhaps allowing Hobo to reach there by Wednesday – appeared to have changed. Overnight the boat rigging rattled and frequent bumps declared the close presence of elemental forces, unruly and contemptuous of my personal sailing plans. At 6am the Irish Met Office issued a small craft strong wind warning for all coastal areas. It appeared my hopes had again been toyed with and I was again left in a quandary. While I could undoubtedly have reached my next planned port in the mixed wind conditions, it would be cold and a physical fight. Another consideration weighed on my mind, did I really want to get stuck in Arklow, another small fishing port with just a very brief entry in the almanac? When sailing around the UK and indeed Ireland, one has to consider the route several legs ahead and my key priority, at this stage, was to get from Dun Laoghaire south, and then across the Irish Sea to Wales. There appeared to me little point in rushing out of Dublin Bay if I couldn’t detect enough settled weather to achieve the next important goal. Lastly, to sail when the Met Office had warned of strong winds could be considered by many, foolhardy. Solo sailors in borrowed yachts need to be conservative – not that sailing around the

UK in a light displacement fin and spade yacht could truly be considered the behaviour of a classic "conservative".

After two days in the Irish Republic I began to question just why I couldn't listen to their second greatest export, namely Terry Wogan? The same radio frequency used in the UK by BBC radio 2, in the Republic of Ireland is occupied by very low-grade radio stations whose broadcasts fail to match the quality of Ireland's chief contribution to a "good morning". Surely it is strange that, on a daily basis, millions of Britons listen to and watch broadcasters born in the Emerald Isle, each one of whom repeatedly proclaims their Irish cultural identity, while in Ireland itself, not only are British broadcasters as rare as sun on a summer's day, but both UK radio and television programmes fail to survive the short passage across the Irish Sea. There is a sort of asymmetrical relationship here. In the Republic of Ireland I couldn't detect any acceptance of foreign accents on the radio or TV, no sounds of Scots, Welsh or English, just Irish.

So, harbour bound, I was forced to become a tourist again and I spent a damp day wandering the streets of Dublin, a wonderful city and one I knew well. Perhaps it was the familiar sense of a capital city, so like parts of London, or maybe it was the rain or my wet feet but by 7pm and after 63 days aboard a small yacht I was aching for escape and the comfort of home. As I watched the huge Seacats depart from Dun Laoghaire harbour I decided I would "jump ship" for a few days and await better weather from home. This decision was confirmed for me when I discovered surely the best bargain in foreign travel – the SailRail ticket from Dun Laoghaire to London Euston for just €35 each way. Truly amazing. So with an easy and cheap journey ahead of me, I secured Hobo and slept well before an early morning stroll across the harbour to take the

11.10 Stena Line Seacat to Holyhead, Wales and onward by train to London.

*10 – 16 July*

My cruise was suspended for seven days while I awaited better weather from the warmth of my London home. During this period the internet was searched for reliable weather information – "state of the art" GRIB files were studied and I sought advice from the Met Office. For all the good it did, I might as well have paid for a Greek augurer to stare into the entrails of a recently dead pigeon. It seems that perhaps I was reliving the folly of a man who searches for someone to tell him what he most wants to hear. Down the millennia Kings and adventurers have consulted seers and oracles, one after another, until they were told the "right" prediction. What I needed to hear from the forecasters, the summer of 2007 and the misplaced jet stream wasn't going to provide.

*17 July – Day 64*

After much futile searching and agonising I returned to Dun Laoghaire from London to rejoin Hobo and, in spite of a more encouraging weather forecast, it rained all day. I started to feel that, for Hobo and I, Ireland had become our Patagonia and, like the great circumnavigator Joshua Slocum aboard his yacht Spray, we were condemned to repeat our struggle over and over again.

*18 July – Day 65. Dun Laoghaire to Arklow IRE. Passage 38 nm, 7:52 hours*

So now returned to my chosen adventure, metaphorically speaking, I again needed to get back on the horse. Waiting in port creates anxiety. I needed to prove to myself I could continue, so I had to leave the seductive yet soporific marina. My desire to make the most of favourable tides led me to depart the marina at 14:00 for what I hoped would be a simple coast hop to Arklow. Along the coast south from Dublin Bay, all the way to Rosslare, there are a series of offshore sand banks and I intended to stay within their protective wall. The drawback of this decision was the tidal currents were stronger in this channel hence my preference to avoid any northerly stream.

After rounding the headland from the bay I pointed Hobo south with the Kish Bank off to port. The breeze, while light, was southeasterly and it was necessary to motor sail to maintain both course and boat speed. Unfortunately by 15:30 the wind backed into the south and freshened. So it was to be a beat against the wind all the way to Arklow. While the tide compensated for the reduced boat speed, the current against wind created an uncomfortable sea state and spray flew. It was cold and bumpy. At 16:30 I still had 25 nautical miles to go and only three more hours of favourable tide.

The sea conditions became more uncomfortable as, first Codling Bank made its presence felt, and then the strangely named India Bank compressed the current against Wicklow Head. I gazed longingly at the town of Wicklow and considered diverting to find a haven for the night and, with hindsight, perhaps that would have been the best decision but I wanted to make better progress after all the lost days at Dun Laoghaire.

Once past Wicklow the chart seemed to suggest a roughly straight line to Arklow but this underestimated the prominence of the remaining headland of Mizen. Although only 19:30 the tide seemed to have turned before the time predicted in the tidal atlas. I was now the wrong side of Mizen Head, beating into the wind and the current was building against me. I short tacked again and again noting the bearings and gradually – very, very gradually Hobo clawed herself around Mizen to reach the shallow bay leading to Arklow. I had become quite tense as I feared I would fail to get Hobo past the tidal "gate" and in consequence I would have had to turn and run back to Wicklow arriving well after dark. Fortunately I just made it and with the engine helping to stem the current, Hobo made forward progress and I gradually relaxed. I could see there were yachts enjoying an evening race off Arklow and their presence helped reassure me that I would be able to follow them "home". At 21:39 just as the light was failing Hobo passed the breakwater entering the Avoca river and while this was a relief, the falling engine revolutions were not. The wind against tide motor sailing had perhaps stirred up more of the diesel fuel "bug" that had tenaciously survived the pumping of the fuel tank and repeated treatments of "poison". With the engine barely ticking over, I turned Hobo into the tiny marina on the starboard side of the river, just sliding in to settle up against the first vacant pontoon. The passage had been more difficult than I had expected and with the re-emergence of the fuel problem I was a less than an happy mariner. Thoughts of Odysseus, summer rain, crazy forecasts and diesel fuel Harpies combined to remove the key adjective from the name "sleeping" bag.

*19 – 20 July. Days 66 – 67 Arklow*

The town of Arklow, like a number of coastal settlements in Ireland, was founded by a Scandinavian warrior and in this case one called Arknell in the 9th century. Later the Norman warlords developed the town and built a castle. Here, as in so many other places, what is now regarded as Irish, is largely the product of invasion and colonial settlement. But whatever the history, Arklow today is a busy town with an attractive bridge and long beach.

At Arklow I reached the point of de profundis – a depth felt and described so well by that Irish exile Oscar Wilde. The weather and my struggle to make sense of the last three weeks combined and this proved to be the lowest psychological point of the whole trip. Here I felt the heavy weight of disillusionment. The 30 hours of rain that at last ceased on July 21st soaked my spirit and I'm sure my outward appearance reflected my internal greyness.

*21 July – Day 68. Arklow to Rosslare. Passage 36 nm, 7:18 hours*

The key issue influencing my decision when to leave Arklow was the weather forecast for the next 48 to 72 hour period. From my harbour on the south eastern Irish coast I wanted to just hop once to Rosslare and then, the next morning, make the big hop across Saint George's Channel to Wales. A favourable 24 hour forecast would not be enough as Rosslare, a popular ferry port, is not a hospitable place for yachts – shame on the harbour and County Wicklow authorities for allowing this situation to continue. Rosslare is the most favourable, that is, the safest point in Ireland for departure or arrival to or from Milford Haven, Wales, yet perversely, there is no visitor's pontoon, mooring buoy or even viable harbour wall available for leisure craft. The almanac even recommends mariners avoid the all-tide Rosslare and sail further on for the more difficult and sometimes dangerous harbour of Kilmore Quay. However, my preference was to take the safer route and avail myself of Rosslare and perhaps "squat" on the outside of a trawler for a few hours rest before heading off to Wales, the fifth country on my tour of the British Isles. So for this reason I needed more than the tiny weather window that had been my lot since leaving Scotland.

The Saturday morning radio and internet information

suggested to me favourable weather was here and that my double leg passage would be possible – I could be in Milford Haven by that Sunday evening.

A phone call to the harbour master at Rosslare confirmed that, despite the lack of information in the almanac, the harbour would be open to leisure craft. He warned of the likely passage of fast Seacats and other ferry traffic but then ships entering and leaving any harbour can always be expected. At 13:35 I headed Hobo out from the breakwater and turned her due south. There was a fair, northeasterly breeze and two reefs were quickly tucked into the mainsail. Apart from the cold, all seemed well and I anticipated a brisk passage. But this was the Irish Sea and the Celtic fates were not yet satiated of their mischief. In 30 minutes the wind had dropped and despite increasing the sail area, Hobo slowed to a slither. If Rosslare was to be reached by dark I would have to motor sail and the 10hp "donked" away at the sea miles. The series of offshore banks and their guard buoys dotted the horizon to port and I occupied myself plotting my progress on the chart. Off Cahore Point I counted 21 huge "wind" turbines – funded by we European Union tax payers – all motionless. Not a watt of electricity being generated. What wind there was had veered from the northeast through east to settle as a light southeasterly. As if to confirm the sometime malevolent nature of the elements, as I neared Wexford, the chart indicated the nearby Lucifer bank. Ancient sailors and fishermen were realists and I can't recall having seen any marine feature on a chart named "happy bank", "velvet race" or "smiling sand".

At 19:52 I called up Rosslare harbour to inform them of my arrival. An easy message to communicate but just where was I to arrive? The sheltered bay suggested welcome but from the sea it was obvious the harbour authorities would rather sailors didn't exist. As previously indicated not a mooring buoy or pontoon was to been seen. The small pair of adjoining harbours, while big enough to accommodate visitor facilities, had bare hard walls and nothing to suggest permission to moor a yacht. Despite expecting this in-hospitality it still rankled, but after a slow circle of the fishing harbour, at 20:44 I berthed Hobo alongside a large trawler named *Motley B*, and hoped that, as tomorrow was Sunday, the "Motley" crew would not be leaving at 03:00 to go fishing. What was needed now was a hot meal and perform the ritual of checking the weather forecast. My meal was satisfying but the forecast quite indigestible. The weather "window" predicted this morning by the forecasters had now disappeared – there was no reference to it or any apology for the error. In its place a southeasterly up to force 7. The course from Rosslare to Milford Haven? Southeast. I felt the spirit drain from my body. What I had tried so hard to avoid while waiting in Dun Laoghaire and Arklow had now happened. I was now to be stuck on Ireland's bottom.

*22 July – Day 69. Rosslare to Kilmore Quay. Passage 19 nm, 3:32 hours*

A disturbed night then followed and a gloomy cold dawn followed that. Given the predicted weather conditions, I could not risk a solo passage of more than 70 nautical miles beating into a force 7 wind. Rosslare was not the place to await a favourable wind so I had no real option but to round Greenore and Carnsore points and make for Kilmore Quay, with its marina and the promise of a comfortable village. So at 07:00 Hobo and I left Rosslare to dodge crab pots and join the strong tidal currents sweeping west along the south Irish coast.

The light wind from the south west was mostly courtesy of the ebb tide so the engine again served to provide propulsion. Crab pots to the left of me, crab pots to the right and pots dead ahead – this was definitely not a passage to be undertaken at night. Tuskar Rock light is the dominating feature on the coast and I imagined the many thousands of mariners who had found comfort in its presence and certainty. Electronic chart plotters may improve still further but all the virtual displays will never replace the heart warming truth of light as seen by human eyes. May Trinity House always provide lights and buoys around our coasts.

First there was Barrel Rocks then Black Rock then the Brandies. Then on the bow the Great Saltee and Little Saltee. This was an obstacle course requiring good pilotage and it re-confirmed my belief that Rosslare is the safer haven for cross channel passages. As the tide turned one hour earlier than the tables predicted I was happy the south easterly near gale had yet to materialise. Subsequently, while internet surfing in safety of my home it was "interesting" to note that an Irish diver's website listed sixty-two identified ship wrecks off Kilmore.

Through the binoculars I found Kilmore Quay and a reassuring procession of Sunday morning angler boats leaving its entrance and indicating the safe leading line of 007 degrees. To get to this point a boat arriving from the east has to cross a narrow gap in the off lying shoals. At 10:00 the strangely named St Patrick's Bridge was found and once across this "hole" in the sand I was able to turn Hobo to the north and ferry glide her in the strong cross current towards the breakwater. At 10:32 I was secured to the pontoon and ready for the predicted strong winds to blow.

Did they blow? Err, well no. Once again the high-priests of so much expensive technology had failed and I was left regretting my decision. This morning had I chosen to ignore the false weather forecast, by nightfall I would have been in Wales. Throughout the day the sun shone and a light southerly breeze tickled those of us in Kilmore harbour.

*23 – 24 July. Days 70 – 71*

The village of Kilmore – population just 417 – proved to be pleasant but consisted of little more than one street; one fish and chip shop, one hotel and one pub. Happily Kehoe's Pub and Parlour proved to be something worth savouring and the line caught, fish of the day "special" consistently delighted this diner. The harbour Master was friendly but despite the boasted marina, there was no shower block or 24 hour toilets. Washing and toilet facilities did exist – at the village Community Centre – but the opening hours were more suitable to the village residents than itinerate mariners.

One of the complications of open water passage making is that of the tides. The simplistic idea of water rhythmically rising and falling doesn't describe the complex movement of water over a distance of, say, 70 nautical miles between two large islands. A successful passage to Wales across St George's Channel by a solo sailor in a small sailing yacht requires several elemental factors happening concurrently. Firstly a fair wind from any direction other than the south east, and, importantly, forecasted not to increase; moderate sea state for what would be at least a 12 hour crossing; enough hours of daylight to allow arrival before darkness; lastly, a tide pattern permitting a yacht to exit from Kilmore and leave the Irish coast on a incoming flood tide and, 12 hours later, arrive on the Welsh coast with the benefit of the next ingoing flood. This aspect of using an incoming tide at the port of arrival was something I'd been "embracing" since leaving the Thames. With an engine that, in a head wind, only managed to push Hobo forward at about three knots, entry to a harbour with a three knot plus outgoing tide was impossible. So for my trip back to the "mainland" I needed to chose my departure date and time carefully. Once a favourable tide pattern had been missed due to forecasts of southeasterly fresh winds, I might have to wait seven days before the cycle of twelve hour tide patterns again became favourable. This was the situation I found myself in while sitting in the cabin at Kilmore towards the end of July.

A week long holiday in southern Ireland must be very relaxing and doubtless every summer many thousands of tourists enjoy their stay. Here's the rub though, when one has a yacht in a harbour incurring a daily charge, an all consuming desire to reach home in the next four weeks, and a passionate compulsion to achieve the self-imposed adventure of circumnavigation, a week in port is not a "holiday" – however irrational it might appear, to me it felt like imprisonment. I was on an escape committee of one and my mind rarely ceased turning over ideas for a break out.

Nonetheless in the mean time I tried to be "normal". On the 24th July a day trip to popular Wexford by bus helped distract me, but, of course, while there, I checked the weather forecast and reconnoitred the riverside for a possible future visit by sea. While the High Street was picturesque and entertaining – at least in comparison to Ardglass and Arklow – the water front was fairly bleak. The almanac had warned ominously that entrance to Wexford from the sea "should not be attempted without local assistance" due to an extensive sand bar and silting. This was one of the reasons I had passed Wexford by and sailed on to Rosslare. However, the almanac also falsely suggested there was a new marina "with all facilities" and the town map repeated this assertion. My personal inspection in summer 2007 revealed the marina as a myth and there was nothing that could welcome a visiting boat larger than a dinghy. Had I chosen

now turned and I was steering 120 degrees and making 6.5 nautical miles each hour towards Wales.

While Wales was still over the horizon I was able to watch Ireland recede. First the "occasional" wind turbine on Carnsore point and then the far more practical Tuskar light grasping tight the rock below. The scenery was pleasant but the cold chill of morning required consumption of food. This cruise had taught me to ignore the nicety of formal meal times. Rather than eating at the conventional times of breakfast, lunch and dinner, at sea I ate constantly – whenever I felt peckish. Food is one of the few comforters available to the solo sailor. Food provides a pleasant sensual diversion and of course, helps provide calorific fuel for the body engine to stave off the cold. Well that was my theory.

The breeze had strengthened so the first reef was tucked in. At least this required something from me and the physical activity helped boost the circulation. Boats can be very hard to sit on and I often daydreamed of heated cockpit seats with soft gel tops. At 07:30 I crossed the traffic separation zone although I did not see any shipping. It was lonely out there but there was still a good northeasterly breeze, Hobo was bowling along and the weak sun suggested warmth later. At 09:30 I had covered 30 nautical miles and now left Irish waters so I took down the courtesy flag. I was back under UK jurisdiction but I felt far from home. Although I was mid-channel it seemed like the Irish language was to be replaced, not by the sound of my home tongue, but by the strident sound of Welsh. The power of the output of the Welsh language radio stations is remarkable and I might suggest far more to do with militant "Celtic" posturing rather than the needs of contemporary consumers of entertainment. If I hadn't realised it before, I now knew, the coast of Wales is still foreign to a sailor from Greenwich onward bound for the Thames.

On the horizon lay Saint David's Head although exactly which piece of grey land was the "head" I couldn't tell. At this point, I was soon to realise, Hobo was a little too far north and I could have freed off her course towards Skomer Island. However, my desire to stay well northwest of the Smalls, a series of notorious reefs well out to sea, meant that I chose to sail more distance than was necessary. Despite the wonderful GPS chart plotter I still preferred to confirm my track over the ground by visual fixes. Consequently at noon, and about the time of slack water, I closed within five nautical miles of South Bishop light. I had crossed what, to me was the "Irish Channel", but noted the nautical chart designated it as St George's. The sun was now a bit warmer and I had started to shed some of my many layers of clothing.

I had now detected the first of the southeast flowing current. Although a little way north of where I needed to be, my strategy had worked fine and I had five hours of favourable tide and was just 10 miles from the mouth of Cleddau estuary. While passage making can at times be full of trial and discomfort, the sheer inner pleasure that seems to accompany a successful landfall is more than any cheap thrill that can be bought at a so called "adventure park" or experienced with a gaming consol. Oh happy day.

With the sails freed off and the current under the keel, Hobo raced ahead towards the gap between Grassholm and Skomer Island. Here was something different. Names that suggested the fashionable "Celtic" chatter of the local radio was again only part of the story. The names of these islands are Norse and evidence that Scandinavian mariners and colonists made this coast home. While today the Welsh tourist board prefers to promote these islands solely as wildlife reserves, the very obvious Norse heritage is sadly largely ignored.

At 13:00 I shook out the reef and, just one hour later, passed Skomer close to port, dodging the Puffins as I went. After tedious hours of non-activity it was now all so different. I turned Hobo to pass though the narrow channel east of Skokholm – Norse for wooded island – and started to encounter various boats with their happy smiling crews enjoying a Sunday afternoon. It seemed as if, after being lost, I had returned to a commonwealth. This felt "unusual". Maybe I was tired and emotional but something "healthy" warmed me inside, it was like the beginning of the summer.

Of course Mr Shakespeare had long ago promoted the benefits of Milford Haven. He saluted it in two plays and in *Cymbeline* floated the questions:

> how far it is to this same blessed Milford.
> And by the way
> Tell me how Wales was made so happy as
> To inherit such a haven
>
> *Cymbeline*, Act 3, Scene 2

This "blessed haven" was now on the bow and at 15:09 I rounded Saint Anne's Head and entered the west channel and Milford. Hobo's average speed under sail from Ireland had been 6 knots and the incoming tide now eased boat with its tired solo crew deeper into this renowned inlet and deeper into Wales.

At first the haven showed its best face – perhaps the face that first millennium Norse mariners would recognise – wooded hills, clean rocky shores and two sandy bays where any longboat could safely come ashore. Then at the haven's first bend, the South Hook Marine Terminal. What is it about petrochemical installations that always manages to turn beauty into a beast? To my eye they are all steel pipes, tanks and girders welded together in an impossible puzzle. There is nothing, just nothing "natural" about them. Whereas sometimes ship wharves and Victorian docks manage to appear to have been "set" into the natural world with a semblance of sympathy, anything associated with the petrochemical industry looks totally alien. Shame, but then this is twenty-first century economics, and the town of Milford was created in response to industry.

The harbour is huge and perhaps big enough for both real beauty and the beast. Hobo, by then under jib alone, coasted forward up river. I was making for Milford Dock with its enclosed marina. The river is wide and the channel well buoyed but, as to be expected, busy with large commercial vessels. The Milford marina is entered by way of a lock and this was not due to open until 16:45. So I was content to slowly sail along, enjoying a mug of tea while dodging the busy tugs and pilot boats.

The marina lock master allowed me to enter as per the schedule and, after a sharp turn to starboard, at 17:01 Hobo was resting comfortably, berthed on a marina pontoon surrounded by impressive Victorian brickwork. The sun shone still warmer and the people on the dockside displayed colourful clothes and smiles, which to me suggested, some sort of joyous holiday had already begun.

*30 July – Day 74. Milford Haven to Dale Bay. Passage 5 nm, 1:32 hours*

After enjoying a rare treat – cooked breakfast, in the sun, at a harbour side café – I visited the marina office and was given a very comprehensive guide to the town and tidal estuary. Yet something in the guide book puzzled me. According to the town council, Milford Haven was founded by whalers from Nantucket. To me this seemed an odd suggestion, particularly since I then knew the Scandinavians had been here in the ninth century, and Shakespeare, in the sixteenth century, had thought the place worthy of a glowing "name check". But I liked Milford so I thought it worth a visit to the library – and of course I was again able to check the internet for weather predictions.

So here is my retelling of the strange limerick, "There was once a man from Nantucket.." According to historians, in the year 1790, a certain Sir William Hamilton, he of Naples, Italy and flirty wife fame, decided there was profit to be earned in Britain by supplying the whale oil previously obtained from New England, which was unfortunately by that date in the new very foreign Republic of the United States. On land in Wales recently inherited, he together with his agent Sir Charles Grenville, proposed building a new harbour and town to attract disaffected American Quaker whalers and their families to settle and run the enterprise. These ex-Nantucket Quakers with names such as Rotch, Folger and Starbuck had, from 1783, migrated from post-independence America transferring their business enterprise to Dartmouth, Nova Scotia, Canada.

Following a protracted period of lobbying the UK government, Sir William at last secured an Act of Parliament allowing both a new harbour and town to be built on the north shore of the river Cleddau. The Quaker whalers, before leaving Canada, insisted that the new town of Milford Haven would include a meeting house and burial ground but also that and their folk would not be required to "embarrass themselves with agricultural activity". So the story of Milford Haven is that Americans, at that time temporary Canadians, came to Wales to become "British" and ran the South Sea Fishery, hunting whales in the Pacific Ocean. This is a story so strange it has to be true. Like so much about the four home nations of these islands, Welsh Milford Haven has a very mixed cultural heritage.

Oh and that Hamilton woman? Lord Admiral Horatio

Nelson visited Milford in 1802 and declared it was one of the finest harbours ever seen, a judgement probably not too greatly influenced by the fact he was having a torrid affair with the wife of the town's patron. Yes, I spent a very pleasant day. I recommend a visit to Milford Haven.

However, although the river and surroundings beckoned me to stay longer, I knew I had to seize the opportunity presented by the strange phenomenon of a weak high pressure weather system. I had to push on and, after a study of the charts, I realised I still had another couple of significant sea passages to make. First I had to cross the Bristol channel to Padstow and, then from there, sail around Land's End and the Lizard.

Padstow, to my concerned surprise – as I have previously declared, prior to the starting the cruise I did no route planning – was 80 nautical miles from Milford Dock and as the Cornwall harbour lay behind an infamous sand bar named The Doom, I would need to arrive near to high water. My calculations led me to conclude I should leave Milford at least four hours before high water and consequently butt the strong foul current all the way out of the river. This was not great, but there was another problem, namely I couldn't lock out of Milford dock at that state of the tide. The solution to the problem was to leave Milford that very evening just before high water and travel down river to Dale Bay, 5 nautical miles nearer the river mouth. At Dale I could either anchor off the beach for the night or alternatively pick up a vacant local mooring. This overnight location would shorten my next day's passage and lessen the amount of foul tide I would have to face.

My decision made, at 18:00 I locked out of the dock and motored west to Dale – a place named using the Norse word meaning "valley". An hour and half later I found a suitable mooring buoy off the beach and settled down to enjoy the evening sunset and, unfortunately, a little less than tranquil anchorage – the frequent ship and tug movements created sufficient wash to rock my dinner table and shake my scotch and soda. I bet those Norse sailors in the ninth century didn't have this problem.

*31 July – Day 75. Dale Bay to Padstow. Passage 75 nm, 14:00 hours*

At 04:15 there was still a full moon lighting the bay and shimmering in the calm water of the anchorage. We English speakers usually apply the word silvery when describing moonlight, but no silver metal has ever shone with such unearthly beauty as the moon. A sublime sight but, unfortunately, something I didn't have the time to fully enjoy. I had many sea miles to go and adrenalin was already stimulating my senses as I readied Hobo for our big push south. At 05:00 I let go the buoy and motored out into the incoming tide. I moved Hobo across to the east side of the channel hoping soon to escape much of the contrary current. High water wasn't until 07:59 but the further I moved south, away from the river entrance, the less negative effect the current would have on my progress. The air was dead calm and I motored with the main sail hoisted ready to help indicate any favourable breeze.

At 06:09 I was abeam Turbot Bank – oh that this prince of fish was still plentiful enough to be a regular on the dinner plates of us Brits. Beginning the day motoring by autohelm, while perhaps unpleasant for the sailing purist, was not too inconvenient. After my hasty awakening I was now able to enjoy a mug of tea and a breakfast sandwich while Hobo chugged on under diesel and electrical power. I sat on the stern rail and surveyed the watery scene. While my cold cheese and pickle sandwich filled the stomach it wasn't the hot bacon I'd have preferred. Somehow I'd never really mastered the preparation of a hot breakfast at sea – something to be learned and practised on my next cruise perhaps.

The Bristol Channel, as with so much of the sea from the Clyde to this point south, was empty. It was just Hobo and me and lots of thoughts. However my main preoccupation was the hope of a breeze. Using binoculars I searched the horizon for any sign that I would soon be truly sailing. It was not until 08:00 that a light easterly started to flutter the mainsail, but it was another two hours before the breeze had gained strength enough for me to silence the engine and sail the boat using just the force of nature. Hobo was making 6 knots and as each hour passed, steadily and without much fuss, we moved away from the coast of Wales and closer to Cornwall.

At 11:00 I was halfway and I could clearly see the Isle of Lundy, 20 miles to the east. It was now warmer and there was bright, bright sunshine. My spirits were higher than they had been for the past thirty days – perhaps summer had at last arrived and maybe the smell and damp of melancholia could at last be blown out of the boat. My seemingly Odyssean adventure had, at last, received new energy and I felt strong, happy and quite silly.

As if to mark my recovered "youthfulness", soon after 13:00, I saw a dolphin, then another and another. Soon I realised that the sea was alive with jumping, flashing blue/grey bodies. I started to count them – always a difficult task – but quickly gave up. I guess there were a hundred or more in this school, all swimming east up against the current. I assume, unseen by me but in clear focus for the dolphin, another less glamorous shoal of little fish was heading the other way – as so much "fast food".

Today when the sea is calm, the world looks deliciously flat. My eyes saw 360 degrees of immense shiny pancake with me at the centre. When the sea is rough and the boat rock and rolls, with creased and broken waves all around, the world appears very small, blurry eyes focusing on just the next few metres of heaving water.

The beauty of the calm sea and the wonderful natural light is something I really savoured, aware that some day soon our deluded Westminster government might have destroyed everything I surveyed. The sea here has been designated as a possible site for 250 wind turbines. The so-called Atlantic Array, if and when built, will stretch from 11 miles off the south Wales coast blocking off a huge forbidden quarter of sea approximately 16 miles wide all the way across the Bristol Channel to just off the cliffs of Devon – a truly vast area where some day boats won't sail and birds won't fly. One day, mariners like myself might not have the freedom to sail in a straight line from Milford Haven to Padstow, as the route will be a killing zone of giant "monuments" to green folly, stuck across the sea bed. With the Atlantic Array the very environment and nature of our coast and sea will be changed forever. I believe now is the time for all sailors to stand up for our right to sail our coastal waters and all true "environmentalists", should speak loudly in defence of our seascape.

By 16:00 I could see land and what I believed was the Pentire Point headland, just off the east of the entrance at Padstow Bay. As always, from the deck of a boat when at sea, it is very difficult to recognise a feature that appears so obvious on the paper chart. A sight angle of just a few degrees changes the perception of what is ahead, however, through the binoculars, the view of small fishing boats moving too and fro helped me pinpoint the headland and differentiate between the Newland – the right side – and the Mouls – the wrong side. As Hobo came closer, the incoming tide rushing along the north Cornwall coast started to have a greater effect than I'd anticipated. It would have been better for me to have arrived further west and, as I neared Newland Rock, I had to fire up the engine to stop Hobo being set away to the east. With a little effort I passed the rock – really more of an island – and at 17:50 entered Padstow Bay. It was about an hour and a half before high water and the grimly named Doom sand bar was visible but thankfully very docile. The chart and almanac both agreed I should head for the east shore and then turn due south at the red Greenaway buoy. Having a 1.7 metre fin keel required me to be a little more conservative than the numerous mackerel boats, steaming at full speed back to harbour to empty their happy holiday makers onto the quayside.

Yellow to the left and yellow to the right, the Camel Estuary is fringed with beautiful yellow sand. After the month of terrible grey weather in Ireland it seemed I had just arrived at a Caribbean paradise. Okay, I may have just been affected by all the unaccustomed sunlight, and this was my first visit to Padstow, but I still believe the place is very special.

As the river narrowed, the number of channel buoys increased and it was important for me to mark my progress, buoy after buoy. At Saint Saviour's Point Beacon the channel divided and the pilot book's instructions were to turn to starboard and steer close to the shore. And when I write "close" I do mean uncomfortably close. I moved ahead at dead slow with a chart in one hand, the almanac in the other, and the tiller between my legs. Soon the outer harbour entrance was visible and between the stone walls I could see into the locked inner sanctum. I wasn't mentally prepared for just how small Padstow harbour was, but thankfully, as I edged forward at dead slow, I knew Hobo was a boat that could spin on a sixpence, and what appeared to be just a few square metres of free water was more than enough. On this Tuesday in July, Padstow harbour was a bustling raft of yachts, all nestling together tied to the quayside – the quayside a seething throng of holiday makers, making the most of the entertainment that so many shiny yachts provided. This was a wonderful welcome for a solo sailor – I felt like I had arrived at a special party and this was a party I really wanted to attend.

At 19:00 Hobo was tidy, albeit rafted four yachts out from the quay, but I was very happy.

*1 August – Day 76. At leisure in Padstow*

At Padstow I, at last, felt like I was truly on holiday, rather than an unwanted vagrant in a boat. The town in summer was alive with the released energy that results from contact with a gathering of people determined to enjoy themselves. The harbour was a Greek theatre stage and the members of the family audience circled, eating and drinking, each person part of the overall comedy. For me the morning was best and, of course, later during the afternoon and evening, the town became quite crowded and commercial. But on a small island such as Britain one has to expect fun places to be popular and Padstow was very popular. The crowds of people I could handle, but the plague of seagulls were just noisy and dirty, resembling a pack of white rats. It's not the sea or the boats that chiefly attract the gulls it's the takeaway food, or rather what is thrown away or just dropped, that the gulls seek. Thousands of seagulls without a natural predator – surely there is some form of "commercial farming" that could harvest and process sea gulls? If it is acceptable to the ecologically minded but pet owning masses for trawlers to catch pretty living fish, merely for use in making pet feed or for soil fertilizer, surely someone could do the same with sea gulls?

Being in a raft of yachts in a crowded small harbour with lock gates is very different from lying to a finger pontoon in a marina. The raft is a social place where the necessity to adjust mooring warps and cross each other's foredecks facilitates dialogue – the other type of intercourse. There is fellowship and the shared experience of the sea, there are smiles and cheerful voices. People ask for and freely offer advice on how to reach the next port of call. Not all the advice is of gold standard but it is all meant well.

Padstow is famous, of course, and has, in the last few years, acquired another valuable tourist attraction to add to harbour, attractive streets, beaches and the river, that of the ubiquitous Rick Stein – celebrity chef. Mr Stein is a sort of Padstow oligarch owning four restaurants, a cookery school, guesthouse, delicatessen, patisserie and even a gift shop. While some natives might grumble about Mr Stein and his many money making enterprises, it is Stein who has "marketed" Padstow to a new class of upwardly mobile visitor – those prepared to spend, at the time of writing, £70 on dinner for one or £8.10 on takeaway cod and chips in a newspaper. The natives of Padstow should sing loud "Long live Mr Stein".

My day at leisure was something I wanted to savour, and I could happily have remained in Padstow for several days more, but my stern mistress, the around Britain cruise demanded action. With so many days misspent due to the poor weather suffered while traversing the coast of Ireland, I had just three weeks to get back to Greenwich. I had to move on and get Hobo around westernmost Land's End and on to the south coast. Here was another ominously named land feature, Land's End and a close study of the charts suggested rounding this peninsular might be a serious challenge – it perhaps representing the Cape Horn of the British Isles.

A skipper of a fin keel yacht like Hobo must carefully consider possible ports of refuge. Hobo's very potent bottom half, her slender pleasing keel, meant she couldn't take to ground in a drying harbour. From Padstow west along the north Cornwall coast there were only drying harbours and this meant, once I left, I would either have to round Land's End or, if encountering strong south westerly winds and bad tide, turn back to Padstow or even flee all the way to Ireland. A long or bilge keel yacht would be able to find shelter in St Ives but this option wasn't available to Hobo, so some careful tidal calculations were required. Calculations to be checked and then checked again. The almanac suggested the tidal current off Land's End can make 4 knots and this combined with the rocks and the unpredictable wind conditions often create dangerous seas. As with rounding any major headland, timing would be the key. The bigger the headland, the more important it is to use any eddies and counter currents. The almanac suggested a west going yacht should aim to pass St Ives at high water Dover and I therefore chose a departure time from Padstow to allow this. It promised to be another long and potentially difficult passage.

*2 August – Day 77. Padstow to Newlyn. Passage 60 nm, 12:45 hours*

Perhaps I was still in holiday mood but, somehow, I missed the early morning radio weather forecast. Not a good start, but while the sky was cloudy and very different from yesterday, there was little to suggest a dramatic change in the weather. At 07:14, an hour before high water I pointed Hobo though the harbour gates and out into the Camel River. I was sad to leave and also quite anxious about what lay ahead. There was a fresh northwesterly wind and an uncomfortable swell that had bulked itself up on the passage across the Celtic sea to form misshapen grey harpies of water. Once beyond the Doom Bar, with one reef in the mainsail and the working jib, Hobo and I close reached west towards Trevose Head. From this point on I knew that I had twelve hours to either round Land's End or re-enter Padstow with the next high tide.

At 08:45 I was just north of Trevose and able to free off the sheets a little and steer a course, bringing the wind slightly more towards the beam. The now ebbing tide increased the speed over ground to largely negate the benefits of the course change. With the apparent wind Hobo's speed was creating, she was still close reaching, and at seven knots it was wet and wild. In fact I was going too fast and at this rate Hobo would arrive at Land's End too early. With more than six hours to go, and no way of knowing what the wind would do next, although concerned, I was not prepared to attempt to slow down. Hobo sped on towards the distant cliffs and famed beaches of Newquay, the onshore wind ensuring that neither was a friendly place for yachts and their crew. After the joy of yesterday while at leisure, today felt very cold and uncomfortable. The sea state while perhaps best described as moderate, was worrying me. Just what would it be like off Land's End? Alone on a yacht you are at the mercy of your thoughts, the real world and the internal mental fantasy image become interdependent. Alone on a yacht the real world sometimes, painfully, reflects the imagination. Remember the legend on the old sea charts of the medieval mariners, "here be monsters"? With six hours to go and nowhere to turn for a haven, I again imagined monsters.

At 10:25, now past the town of Newquay, I put a second reef in the mainsail, although this didn't seem to have much effect on Hobo's speed or motion. The course from Trevose Head to off St Ives was 235 degrees and, in effect, a straight line. While I could not see ahead that far into the distance, I knew St Ives was there, no course changes were needed, just a close reach. In the last hour Hobo had covered eight miles and I was then certain I would arrive early at the first turning point off Pendeen Head. With St Ives just visible in the distance, I dropped the main and sailed on with just the jib. Psychologically this was painful – as a racing sailor it felt sacrilegious to intentionally slow down a yacht – and physically it was painful as the boat motion increased and the swell now tossed the underpowered Hobo about. Happily the cloud was by then breaking up and occasional sunny spells improved the previously threatening look of the coastline. Lots of yellow sand and St Ives now looked more attractive than it had on paper. If only the town had, like Padstow, invested some of their local taxes to provide a better harbour with lock gates.

The Stones Reef marked the east side of St Ives Bay, and had the wind been from the southwest, I would probably have chosen to tuck Hobo into the west corner, just off Carbis Beach, and awaited the tide. However, the onshore northerly wind made this inadvisable so I had to push on.

Sailing under jib alone irritated me, so early arrival at Land's End or not, I re-hoisted the mainsail. Hobo felt better and to me at least, she looked better. Not that anyone else could admire her as, yet again, Hobo was the only boat at sea and this increased my suspicion that everyone else knew something that I didn't. Hobo was the only boat on this sea, too early for the tide and alone in heading towards Land's End.

As the tide was then against me and would be all the way around Land's End, I moved Hobo closer in to the coast. There would be a slight contrary stream close in to the cliffs but just how close is too close? Where there are cliffs there are usually underwater rocks, but close was the advice in the pilot book, so close I went. At 14:00 I was practically close enough to collect sea weed off the rocks as Hobo crept by Zonnor Head, just out of the tide, but skimming the seabed, and dodging the usual crab pots.

And then it happened. For the previous eight hours sailing along the north Cornwall coast it had been windy, cold and uncomfortable but then suddenly, at 15:20 just ahead of the first corner – Pendeen Head, a corner on the edge of England – the sun came out, the sea calmed and the wind decreased. The monster I had visualised, vanished. All I could do was laugh, start the engine and steer Hobo close to the rocks and inside the non-existent watery over falls. To increase my delight, at last I had company – a forty foot yacht bound from Ireland and now on my course around Land's End.

The sea, although boiling due to the currents in all the places the chart indicated, largely became greasy and gentle. The current tore at the underwater hills and weed beds but on the surface Hobo motor sailed with a following wind, upright and with a dignified sexy sway like a runway fashion model in high heels. On the land, long abandoned tin mines full of ghosts and bats, dotted the green cliff tops, but far below, on the water, at 16:28 Hobo passed Cape Cornwall and outside Brissons Rock. Oh how different this would be in a southwesterly gale.

Next came Whitesand's Bay but, unfortunately, while I enjoyed the visual beauty, the VHF radio provided a touch of harsh reality. The marine channel alerted listeners with a sombre one-sided commentary on search and rescue attempts to find two missing divers further along the coast. At first I was confused due to the coastguard reporting the search was in Whitsand Bay. I looked around me and wondered if there was anything I could do to help. But the desperate scene was not here, it was further on at a dive site nearer Plymouth. The divers were eventually found but sadly too late. The sea is magnificent but not our natural element, and we all trespass, knowing the delights and the risks. But for me though it was all bright sunshine and sparkling water, a fair tide and a following breeze – probably about as good as it gets.

Up on the cliff tops I watched the crowds of tourists in T-shirts, enjoying the "delights" of Land's End with its pub, gift shop and opportunities for spending money. I believe Hobo must have provided a pleasant addition to the vista for spectators as, at 17:25, we passed by close to the shore and over Kettle's Bottom and inside the Long Ships reef with its "ivory" lighthouse.

Off to starboard and four miles to the southwest was Wolf Rock lighthouse and what I assumed was a supply helicopter, buzzed overhead. All very scenic and so very different from what I had been expecting on the long sail down the Cornish north coast.

Ahead of me lay the last significant corner of the day, Gwennap Head with its offshore Runnell Stone Reef, this my furthest point south and, at 18:17, I was a happy sailor as I steered Hobo east northeast. At last I truly felt I had passed the major obstacle blocking my entry onto the south coast. I had rounded Britain's "Cape Horn". To add to my delight the wind filled, perhaps freed of all complications posed by the confused land mass of Land's End. The engine was again silenced and Hobo beam reached along the coast and towards Mounts Bay and the numerous white specks that suggested the yachting folk of Penzance were at play. While Penzance for the night was an attractive thought, I knew my plan tomorrow was to push onward around the Lizard. If I made for Penzance I would have to enter the wet dock and be "imprisoned" there until around high water – inconvenient if I wanted to carry the flood tide east around the Lizard and up to Falmouth. So big Penzance was off and little Newlyn was definitely on. Despite the almanac's description for Newlyn, a friend had told me there were now pontoon visitor berths available at the fishing cooperative, and this seemed by far my best option for the night.

By comparison with the last few harbours on my cruise, Newlyn was easy to find and easy to enter. After rounding the south pier, the pontoons of the fishing Coop were straight ahead. At 20:00 Hobo was secure for the night. It had been, at times, a day of anxiety – lasting until mid-afternoon and that was more than long enough. I think I had earned my scotch and soda.

*3 August – Day 78. Newlyn to Falmouth. Passage 36 nm, 6:56 hours*

Somehow or other, perhaps in the satisfying emotional glow of having rounded Land's End, and maybe due to effects of too much sun and a celebratory whisky, I'd made a mistake with my tidal calculations. Perhaps not too foolishly I'd assumed because there was a convenient Falmouth high water at nine in the evening and Falmouth was to the east of me, I would have all morning in Newlyn to relax and explore. Fortunately, as I munched my early breakfast muesli, I rechecked the tidal atlas and to my chagrin realised I'd made a mistake. I was correct about the time of high water but wrong about the direction of flow around Mounts Bay and around the Lizard. If I wanted to have a favourable easterly tide for the Lizard I needed to leave Newlyn immediately and pass the Lizard by noon.

So regrettably I didn't get to enjoy a full cooked breakfast at the Fisherman's Mission or inspect yet another silly plaque marking a claimed stop off for that ubiquitous little ark of malcontents, the Mayflower.

At 07:40, with the cabin in some disorder, I left the harbour and motored out into a calm and sunny bay. With the autohlem on steering duty, I made ready for sea and made another mug of tea – the Englishman's cure-all following moments of adversity.

While it had been an unpleasant rush to leave, I knew today I had just 36 nautical miles to cover and this, when compared with the last thee long sea legs, was an absolute "doddle". And there was the sun, something that had, for much of the last 75 days, been such a rarity. I felt as if this, at last, was really summer and the type of weather, in any normal year, we Brits can expect. And in addition, to brighten my humour even more, there was the company of other little vessels. Whereas, since leaving the Clyde, with the exception of Dublin Bay, I had sailed on an empty lonely sea, now on the south coast of England, in every direction little boats tracked from all points of the compass. I had joined an unofficial but joyous regatta. I had to restrain myself from adopting the Swedish protocol of waving to each and every boat as I passed.

A southwesterly breeze sped Hobo towards the Lizard and I peered through the binoculars searching for any sign of the Boa or the other tidal over falls indicated by the chart. Naturally perhaps given the wind conditions and state of the tide, the race off the Lizard was nothing more than a few bubbles rather than any boat crunching maelstrom. My passage track had however, been chosen as I left Newlyn, so at 10:30, a very safe 5 nautical miles south of the Lizard, I turned Hobo northeast. Another day and another British headland ticked off from my list.

And now another first, with the sun bright and the air temperature positively summer, I swapped my sailing uniform of fleece and thermals for just shorts. A pale, almost mildewed human body, topped by a wizened, weathered head – I must have looked something like George Orwell's character Winston Smith in 1984 after several months in his prison cell. Certainly I was not the bronzed, ruggedly healthy looking male of the Saga holiday advertisements. Yet despite the exterior visage, inside I was content and surprisingly fit considering the past 77 days of adventure.

By 12:30 the ebb tide had reached Hobo and progress slowed as I avoided the Manacles Reef then showing above the surface of the water. As I stared at the sea, thinking of the grip of the keel ripping reef and wondering how many brave ships had been held fast, a huge floppy tail fin slapped the water alongside. Leaping to my feet I saw the long muscular body of a Basking shark as it gave a few lazy "kicks" to move out of my way. I'd disturbed lunch but only for a second. Then a safe distance behind Hobo, the Basking's dorsal and tail still showed and I watched, fascinated as to how it could be a creature so large can be sustained by mere plankton.

Ahead of Hobo lay the hotels and buildings of Falmouth. Pendennis Point and Saint Anthony's Head were easily recognisable and a quick course correction put Hobo on line for Saint Mawes. While this was my first visit to Falmouth from the sea, to me all the names were very familiar. It is impossible to read any book written about the seafaring history of Britain without coming across reference to this superb haven and maritime community. Carrick Roads is a place where one might expect to find square rigged sailing ships at anchor. If only the UK and its institutions valued our collective maritime history then perhaps, like so many of the Baltic States, we would have a fleet of glorious sail training ships – maybe a working replica of a Lisbon Packet or perhaps a "living" and breathing Cutty Sark. At 14:02, as I passed Black Rock, regrettably there was nothing that magnificent, just a couple of seagoing tugs. The sun had gone and had been replaced by a damp light drizzle. From Falmouth's many safe marinas I chose the visitor's Yacht Haven – the closest mooring point to the town's main street. Shielded from view by both swinging moorings and yachts at anchor, I threaded Hobo between all the boats until the visitor pontoons were revealed and immediately behind them, the old quay and Customs House. It felt to me as if I was reliving a little piece of what the sailors down the centuries had experienced, but then, perhaps surprisingly considering the hardships, sailing is a pastime of a romantic. At 14.36 the engine was silenced and Hobo allowed to rest until tomorrow.

Happily it was still early and I had all afternoon to explore a very busy Falmouth and, importantly, try and replenish the "ships stores". I hoped to find things just as colourful as Lord Byron had, when as visitor in 1809, he wrote, "Claret is good, and Quakers plentiful, so are herrings salt and fresh" – not sure what I would do with Quakers but wine and fish would have been welcome.

*4 August – Day 79. Falmouth to Plymouth. Passage 42 nm, 7:39 hours*

I had now been on this adventure since 8th May and the proverbial clock had begun clicking ever louder in my ear. I had to restart paid employment on 28th August and I had always planned to have Hobo back to Greenwich well before then. While there was a little over three weeks left, I was running out of time. It seemed to be a cruel fate to have arrived on a beautiful part of Britain's coast, where every few miles there exists a deepwater harbour with colourful town and, at last, the weather fit for pleasure, yet to be so short of time. Time cannot be turned back however, and although I was frustrated to be leaving, at 07:40 I let go the pontoon and set off once more, this time towards Plymouth.

The simple plan, as always, was to carry a favourable tide, keeping the coastline on my left – easy. The sun of yesterday had been exchanged for heavy grey clouds and a damp cold mist but at least I knew today's sail would be a shortish hop and Plymouth Sound provided a entrance that even captain Pugwash's cartoon parrot could find.

With a smile on my face I looked across the harbour to Carrick Roads and chanted what I could remember of that Byron poem so full of "salt" and departure:

Huzza! Hodgson, we are going,
Our embargo's off at last
Favourable breezes blowing
Bend the canvass o'er the mast,
From aloft the signal's streaming
Hark! the farewell gun is fired,
Women screeching, tars blaspheming,
Tell us that our time's expired
Here's a rascal
Come to task all
Prying from the custom-house;
Trunks unpacking
Cases cracking
Not a corner for a mouse
Scapes unsearched amid the racket,
Ere we sail on board the Packet.

*Lines to Mr Hodgson*, 1809

I put Hobo onto autohelm and cleared the warps and stowed the fenders below preparing the boat for sea. St Anthony's Head marked the way out into the English Channel and the engine was soon silenced as a southwesterly breeze filled the full mainsail and working jib. With a healthy speed of 6.1 knots through the water, despite the poor visibility, I had a smile on my face. Dodman Point was soon passed and at 10:00 Hobo was 7 nautical miles due south of Fowey. When imagining a long hot summer I'd hoped to visit this beautiful Cornish town, but after 78 days surviving un-seasonal weather suitable for nightmares and rabid "climate" change campaigners, I had little time to spare on pleasant tourism. I feared more bad weather and this drove me to cry "eastward ho" and rush ever on.

As the midday sun started to break though the cloud, Rame Head appeared on the bow, decorated, it seemed, by scores of little white sails all heading out of Plymouth Sound for their weekend escape. After often sailing on a lonely deserted sea, the sight of so many boats warmed my heart but plagued my navigation – with so much sea water how can dozens of boats all be on converging courses?

The only problem for mariners entering Plymouth is, perversely, the very thing that makes the harbour safe – the huge offshore breakwater. From the sea a mariner clearly sights the green Hoe in the distance and the white buildings of the Citadel while missing, in the foreground, the mile long low rubble of the Victorian breakwater running like a tripwire across a threshold.

As I sailed into grand Plymouth Sound I thought of Sir Francis Drake and his Golden Hind that, on September 1580, sailed back into their home port, the circumnavigation complete, 1017 days after they had left. What is so often glossed over in all the tedious, mainstream interpretations of UK history, is that this son of a itinerate Devonshire shearman led a small crew of hardy sailors and together this "working class cooperative" navigated a small sailing ship around the world. He was the first man of any nation to achieve this – Plymouth to Plymouth. A worthy national hero. And to help all of you with the next pub quiz, that famous Mr Magellan. while strangely sometimes credited with a circumnavigation, though a great navigator, was very weak on diplomacy and cutlass rattling. He was killed during his voyage in 1521 by natives of the Philippines and therefore, unlike dashing Drake, only completed half the globe. A very different voyage for me but the master mariners of old were never far from my thoughts.

At 13:00 I rounded Penlee Point and gybed Hobo to the north and closed in towards the aptly named Drake's

Island. The city of Plymouth offers yachtsmen a number of options for mooring but, as it was a Saturday night, I decided to head away from the busy centres and hoped for peace and quiet on the river Plym at Yacht Haven. While most visitors seemed to be making for the Barbican or Queen Anne's Battery, I steered across their wakes and headed up river, seeking out an entrance far along the bobbing wall of marina pontoons. At 14:39 Hobo lay once more against a friendly piece of wood.

With the sun then on my back and a good part of the day still unused, I could, of course, have pushed on to Salcombe or Dartmouth but this would have been against my own self-imposed rules – sail with the tide and keep it simple. Continuing eastward would have meant butting the ebb tide and with the weather still highly uncertain – bless the grey nerds of Met Office – I might find myself harbour bound in Salcombe if things went all "Michael Fish".

After a clean up and a snooze I attempted to find meaningful civilisation on the south bank of the Plym – a shop or a restaurant was my quest, but I failed. Yacht Haven proved to be good marina but a little too far from the madding crowd. So my dinner was from the dwindling ships stores and therefore a little less than I hoped for. As I ate my pasta – surely the modern day equivalent of Nelson's hardtack – I reflected on the heavy fact that in 78 days of sailing, Plymouth was the very first harbour I had previously visited by boat. All the ports before had been new to me, but from this point onward, I had the comfort of knowing much of what lay ahead I had encountered before – at least once.

*5 August – Day 80. Plymouth to Dartmouth. Passage 35 nm, 7:06 hours*

A bright and sunny morning stirs the spirit and hastens a sailor to sea. So after a mug of tea and the important first chocolate biscuit of the day I rushed out to catch the tide. I was doubly excited this morning for this day I was bound for one of my favourite places on this planet – Dartmouth. I spent my youth in South Devon and the majestic natural theatre that is the river Dart was an early discovery. The excitement first felt as a whelp has lasted the years and outlived many of the more corporal trophies that may be said to mark a man.

At 07:37 the engine struggled for its first breath of the day, not unlike a smoker after the first drag of Raleigh's revenge. My love hate relationship with this little Volvo was such that every time it started I couldn't help wondering whether today it would finally exhaust the "resident evil" of the diesel tank and prove itself better than so many kilos of fiendish green Swedish metal. Oh yes, the engine did, at times, feel like the proverbial albatross.

Leaving Plymouth via the Eastern Channel requires a skipper to truly wake-up and stop admiring the view. The first 4 nautical miles of the passage east is quite shallow and fringed by nasty keel catching rocks. While my second mug of tea was still steaming I had to guide Hobo around Duke Rock, inside East Tinker and outside the Shag Stone and Mewstone Ledge, this was almost like changing tube lines during the rush hour on the way to work – almost. Just for the record, there a lot of Mew stones around our island and apparently in old English a mew is a seagull – that explains it all.

There was just a very light breeze curling along the coast and, of course, exactly from the direction in which I was headed. Nevertheless, by 08:40 I was abeam of the Mewstone and from this point there was a clear course across Bigbury Bay to Bolt Head. Time for more tea. A gentle swell ensured the sound of constant clanging as everything able to swing, swung – a rhythmic accompaniment to the diesel thud, but all in all, it was a great morning. At 11:30 I was due south of Salcombe and heading for Prawle Point, the second most southerly mark of the circumnavigation.

Just west of the infamous Salcombe Bar is Moor Sand with its fascinating story. Here local divers have found gold – Barbary pirate gold, ah harrrr – 400 or more "Moorish" gold pieces dating from about the year 1630. The scholarly theory is that a Barbary pirate ship was wrecked here while on a raiding mission to capture English slaves for export to the markets of north Africa. The written record of Cornwall and Devon include many reliable Civic reports of raids by North African Barbary Coast pirates causing village after village to become emptied of English men, women and children. An interesting fact to supplement all the usual orthodox theory about Britain which the BBC chooses to propagate.

The headland of Start Point – start of what one might ask? – a sort of speed bump to the east bound current and waves, usually creates ugly, broken water capable of upsetting the unwary sailor. This day however, Hobo skipped her way through and soon the expanse of Start Bay opened out to the north. The sea calmed and the sun reflected a dazzling light show. I hid behind my sunglasses and bared a lot of damp flesh in tribute to the power of nature – okay I just wanted a bit of sun tan after so much mildew.

The 3 nautical mile long Skerries Bank stretched in a line to the northeast, directly in my track, but today the sea merely poured over the shoal rather than bucked and boiled so, at 13:00, I silenced the motor and Hobo drifted on the current, slowly towards, my childhood memories.

Dartmouth is a town and a harbour hidden behind rolling green hills, but the obelisk type beacon just to the east gives the clue to its whereabouts. A first time visitor has to act with confidence and dare to get real close to the shore before an entrance becomes visible. On a leading line of due north, a pair of "pocket" castles suggests to any mariner a town where the inhabitants expected the arrival of raiders cloaked in foreign flags intent on doing evil. The town's archive tells some of the story – Dartmouth was a gathering place for ships to embark on the second Crusade in 1147 – first stop the siege of Moorish Lisbon. Geoffrey Chaucer, of Canterbury Tale fame, visited in 1373 on a mission from the King to discourage the local tradition of "piracy", and in 1592, Sir Walter Raleigh's prize, a Spanish spice ship the *Madre de Dios* was substantially looted by happy enterprising town folk. Dartmouth harbour is a watery temple to seafaring and any mariner instinctively feels at home here. For me though the feeling of home was much more personal. At 15:07 Hobo was secure in a raft of visiting craft at Kingswear's Darthaven marina.

*6 August – Day 81. Dartmouth*

A day for R&R and enjoying the happy smiles of family visitors who, thankfully, one by one appeared on the quayside. Yet there can be little rest for a sailor who has a voyage still to complete and unfortunately the Met Office supplied all the necessary gobbledegook to ensure my mind was cluttered and only partially in social mode. Also there was the engine's fuel system to again purge and bleed. My arrival the day before had, once more, been made difficult by the engine losing power just as I was berthing. To all Yachtsmen, I sadly predict a dangerous future using marine bio diesel with its hidden contagion sure, at some point, to spread to your once pristine and happy fuel tanks.

As I prepared my next day's passage plan I pondered that in the last eight days, I had sailed solo 324 nautical miles, while over the previous twenty-nine days, I had managed a meagre 284. My travails on the coast of Ireland haunted me and in consequence I felt a compulsion to push on quickly with single-minded determination to reach the Thames.

*7 August – Day 82. Dartmouth to Poole. Passage 75 nm, 14:23 hours*

At 04:15 my alarm announced reveille and, although all was dark and cold, I readied Hobo for another day – and this would be a long day. At 05:00 the diesel engine abused the peace of the river and I let go the warps and steered the route taken by countless small craft over the millennia. Down the river and out to sea on a course of 075 degrees across the wide Lyme Bay. There are 43 nautical miles of sea from the Dartmouth Homestone buoy to Portland Bill and, for a deep keel yacht like Hobo, few viable opportunities for a haven should the weather turn hostile. At a speed of 5 knots it would be more than eight hours before I had a chance to use the coast. The choice for me was simple, push on all the way to Weymouth or Poole or, in adversity, turn back for Dartmouth or Torbay. My plan was to push on and try to make Studland Bay off Poole before the arrival of a force 6 wind from the north or northwest predicted by the Met Office.

Of course, with a passage of potentially more than fourteen hours, I would have to abandon my rule about avoiding sailing against the tide. My passage plan allowed that I would butt the foul stream where it was weakest, that is in Lyme Bay, and then arrive off Portland Bill as the tide turned in my favour, the current speeding me on along the Dorset coast and into Studland Bay. That was the "clever" plan, but the breeze wasn't doing me any favours, light and northeasterly, so it was motor sailing. I needed to keep to my schedule if I was to catch the tide off Portland Bill.

At 07:20 I altered course to avoid the Torbay lifeboat with its long towline, on the end of which was a "disabled" yacht dangling like a large mackerel on a spinner. Not exactly "Preservation of Life from Shipwreck" as per the charter of the Royal National Lifeboat Institute, given the calm sea, but perhaps, a sign of the times. Here was a substantial and seaworthy sailing yacht considered to be "in distress" merely because its engine had failed and thereby unable to meet the skipper's diary commitments. Is this really what the RNLI was established for? Perhaps the "distressed" yacht had an attack of diesel bug and "there but for the grace of god, go I" – although, of course, they still had mast, sails and "wind power". Over the VHF radio Brixham Coast Guide re-broadcast a strong wind warning from the Met Office. However, at this moment a little more wind – from the right direction – would have been very welcome.

My routine was soon established, each hour on the hour I plotted my position onto the paper chart and noted my latitude and longitude in the log book. Hour after hour the grey pencil crosses on the chart marked my progress across the light blue coloured paper, the constant blue contrasting with the real life ever changing colours and vapours that is an hour spent at sea. By 10:30, happily, I was more than halfway to the Bill and moving past the halfway point is always a psychologically satisfying transition.

Mid-Lyme Bay is a boring place. Although it may appear a stupid thing to observe, there is just nothing there. Whereas on a channel crossing of 70 nautical miles from England to France a yachtsman encounters the exciting marine motorway type traffic provided by the two busy shipping lanes, in Lyme Bay there is nothing, no ships, no seagulls, just sea.

By 12:30 the tide started to turn in my favour and on the port bow was the stony hump of Portland Bill. At 13:00 Portland Coast Guard repeated the Strong Wind Warning

– force 6 from north northwest. But where I was, 8 nautical miles southwest of the Bill, there was nothing to fill the sails but the apparent "false" wind of Hobo's forward motion. Eventually at 13:53 the red ensign on the stern began to lift and a light northwesterly created a satisfying bit of heel to the boat.

Sadly this wonderful coastal seascape and important sailing route is yet another that will one day be "re-developed" by a Government policy that of using taxpayer's money to fund more of their "fig leaf" wind turbines. All the sea I viewed off the starboard bow will, perhaps from 2016, be littered with concrete and steel towers – taxpayer funded yacht traps with associated restrictions on our historical freedom to sail. I wonder what Drake or Nelson would say.

Returning to the happy present I obeyed the pilot book's recommendation and headed 5 nautical miles south of the Bill and, as this position dictated an east bound sailing yacht should pass to the south of the Shambles sand bank, I scanned the horizon for black and yellow buoys. While passage planning it at first seemed a more inshore track would be beneficial, however, the tidal current is strongest out away from the coast and a course from south of East Shamble to south of Anvil Head avoided the uncomfortable tidal over falls off St Alban's. So with the breeze filling I was at last able to silence the engine and feel Hobo surge under nothing more than the pressure of the wind. With the passing of Portland Bill came the excitement from knowing – and yes seeing – that the coast of Dorset was ever so gradually moving to the left as I sailed closer and closer toward the end of the day and a well earned rest.

But Poseidon or perhaps a Met Office drone dictated that my rest be postponed. By 16:00 I could see storm clouds to the north somewhere up over the Hampshire's New Forest. The towering dark mass of cloud didn't bode well but I couldn't really complain – it had been forecast to arrive at some point and given, in the summer of 2007, the Met Office's almost total inability to provide an accurate forecast, it served as tiny, tiny vindication. As I sped on, sailing a close reach to the northeast, I noticed yachts coming towards me on a full run – they had easterly wind. At this point I sensibly did what all sailors are supposed to do, I shortened sail before the squall arrived. From here my logbook became a blank page – not because of any laziness on my part but because a solo sailor sometimes has more than enough to do. Two reefs were tucked into the mainsail and I quickly pulled full wet weather gear over my shorts and T-shirt. It's a pity I didn't get time to pull on my rubber boots. Suddenly the wind whooshed down and across from the north. Heavy rain accompanied the wind and visibility reduced to barely a mile, not that, with all the cold water in my eyes, I could focus for more than a second or two. Yee ha! The strong wind had arrived and I was fully stretched to hold Hobo on a course for Anvil Head. The cockpit floor was sloshing with rain water and my bare feet started to look and feel less than adequate for the conditions. Ludicrous as it may seem to a non-sailor, I had a broad grin on my face and, like King Lear, I loudly shouted my encouragement to the elements. Here was I being blasted by the wind and water after more than twelve hours at sea and I was laughing at the silliness of it all. Pure boyish fun.

I still had tide in my favour, and having rounded close under the cliff at Anvil Point, there were just the bays of Swanage and Studland to cross. It was then I abandoned my plan of a night at anchor in Studland Bay. Despite the best of Henri Lloyd I was soaked and the wind direction suggested a night off the beach in Studland wouldn't be as restful as I hoped. So, as landmark Old Harry stack, chalky and tall as ever, seemed to point me in the direction of Poole, I took the hint and sailed up the Swash Channel and into the boating paradise that is Poole Harbour. After negotiating the winding channel avoiding ferries and the evening racing fleet, and coping with a silly minor wound, the result of cold fingers on sharp shackles – quickly wrapped in kitchen towel and bound with electrical tape – at 19:23 I tied Hobo to a very posh piece of new pontoon at the Quay Boat Haven marina. One wet, windblown and tired but very self-satisfied sailor.

*8 August – Day 83. Poole to Lymington. Passage 26 nm, 4:15 hours*

Poole proved to have a very busy harbour side, a place where yelling and puking seemed be considered acceptable behaviour for young people. Of course it was August and the holiday season. Nevertheless Poole, with its sheltered expanse of water dotted with thousands of boat moorings, provided the type of marine spectacle that is hard not to enjoy despite the prodigious charges levied on overnight visitors. So after a "full English" breakfast, courtesy of a local café, at 10:53 I departed the marina and piloted Hobo towards the sea. The bright summer sunshine was almost strong enough to induce memory loss of so much grey sky – almost enough. Alas the wind however, was a cold blast from the north, so as usual for a Brit sailor in the summer, I was dressed in a fetching assortment of now well-worn Polartec. The day's passage was to be a mere quick hop compared to the more than fourteen hours of yesterday. Lymington was the destination and although I could easily have made Portsmouth, I had personal reasons for wanting to revisit a town from which I had been absent for thirteen years.

The passage from Poole to Lymington was probably the simplest trip I had undertaken so far. After following the channel buoys and the procession of departing craft, once past the Sand Banks car ferry, one can easily see the white chalk stacks that are the Needles on the Isle of Wight – and the navigation task nearly over, just point the bow at the outer most stack. While this could have been my plan, I chose the slightly more "involved" route, using the north channel entrance to the Solent off Keyhaven. The fresh northerly wind and the short distance allowed me to set just the working jib and I beat leisurely across Christchurch Bay. Hobo sped forward and it was a short 12 nautical miles to the North Head buoy where I turned to the southeast, close to the piled shingle which protects the mainland from the worst of the predominately southwesterly waves. Soon the strong current grabbed the hull and Hobo was shot into the Solent like an olive pip spat into a bucket.

Hurst Narrows, the entrance to the Solent, always fascinated the child in me. The power of all the English Channel tide being forced through a small gap creates whirl pools and a surreal look to the surface of the water. In its way it is far more dramatic than the infamous Straits of Messina off Sicily, and all it would need is for some English language Homer to create a legend of a ship devouring Scylla monster, and any passage through Hurst would be twice as exciting.

As the sheltered waters of the Solent opened before me I could see the telltale white blobs of the two Lymington to Yarmouth car ferries shuttling back and forth just 2 nautical miles away. Therefore to find the entrance to Lymington river one just has to watch the ferries and steer a course to arrive on the north bank at the point where the ferry enters the salt marsh. These marshes and the walled pens that were industriously built, at one time provided Lymington with its major industry. Long before Jamie Oliver, Gordon Ramsay and other celebrity chefs, sea salt was the product of choice to preserve food, but the salt industry closed in 1865, and today it is yachting that provides cash for the local economy. Lymington River is one large bobbing boat park, a premier centre made more valuable by Lymington's all weather and tide access and close proximity to the cross channel route to Normandy. This convenience was well regarded by our continental cousins and on no less than three occasions raiders from France arrived and robbed and abused the locals then burnt the town to the ground – perhaps not too different from today apart from the burning bit. Soon Hobo's jib was down on the deck and I was following the channel markers up the worryingly shallow Lymington River and at 16:08 the passage was completed and I looked forward to a good dinner and a quiet night at Yachthaven.

*9 August – Day 84. Lymington to Gosport. Passage 19 nm, 4:13 hours*

For those who don't already know, the first week of August is always the annual Cowes Regatta Week, and early in the morning, I was aware of the arrival of racing crews on nearby boats. Cowes and the race start line is about two hours away and all around me bright shorts and mirrored sunglasses "danced" as shiny boats were laced with ribbon like, coloured sheets. Medieval knights gathering before a joust couldn't have offered spectators more of a visual carnival. A sunny day, but a day not well suited to yacht racing – wind was sadly absent.

I spent the morning revisiting the town and marvelling at the great selection of marine services, normal for the Solent area but a treasure-trove for a deprived sailor like myself who is based on the Thames, and relies on corporate owned retailers in Britain's largest city.

My passage plan for the day was to have a leisurely sail to Gosport and Portsmouth which I hoped would serve me as an ideal departure point for Friday's longer passage to

Brighton. Disturbingly, when I switched on my previously trusty Garmin GPS chart plotter, the "magic" chip hidden inside reset its memory, wiping all the settings and, more significantly, the entire 1600 nautical mile passage record from Limehouse to Lymington. I can only assume I had filled the memory chip to capacity and to continue to function, the Garmin had simply "cleared" itself. This was a minor irritant as in reality the Garmin 450 had been a wonderful tool, and for a solo sailor, something I now regard as vital for safety.

By lunchtime the staff of Yachthaven were being a little, shall I say, "dogmatic". Despite having paid the most expensive berthing charge I had encountered throughout my entire circumnavigation, I was told that if I didn't leave the marina by 12:30 I would be charged for an additional night. It seems some marinas regard the visitor rate as covering just the night period and not a 24 hour period. So after a smiling orderly visited Hobo, and then a verbal reminder via the VHF radio, at 12:30 I started the engine and glided away from lovely Lymington.

Out on the Solent there was a light easterly breeze but a favourable tide so Hobo, with full sail, looked very much at home as she beat towards the gathering fleet of racing yachts off Cowes. Sadly the breeze was fickle but by a combination of ghosting and drifting Hobo covered the sea miles until we were off the Prince Consort cardinal. The sight of so many hundreds of racing yachts circling the starting line of the Royal Yacht Squadron at Cowes should have been pure pleasure but what with the all the yachts, the frequent Red Funnel ferries and the Brambles Bank, I needed to concentrate to avoid collisions.

At 14:56 I decided that, given the loss of wind and difficulty steering, good seamanship required I turn on the engine. A turn of the ignition key produced nothing but the sound of the starter motor whirring. The Volvo engine wouldn't start and Hobo was drifting sideways in the tide amidst the vast racing fleet, each of which was seemingly ready to call "starboard" at any moment. Given the circumstances and the recent experience of the dreaded diesel bug it was perhaps reasonable for me to jump to the conclusion that the evil bug was stopping the engine. So this solo sailor dived below deck and grabbed spanners, screw driver and paper towels rushing to find the blockage and perform CPR on the sick Volvo. Over the next 30 minutes I blew out fuel lines – watched yachts approaching – bled air from fuel system – shouted apology to right of way yachts – reconnected all fuel lines – worried at the approach of a Red Funnel ferry and only then did I catch sight of the engine decompression lever in the cockpit – "fully out" whereas, of course, it should have been "fully in". With a mixture of horror and humour I reset the decompression lever, started the engine and eased Hobo safely out of the track of several dozen incoming boats. I'm quite sure during that fraught 30 minutes more than a few skippers and crew cursed at the seemingly drifting unmanned yacht and loudly proclaimed on the status of my birth.

Excitement then over, the East Solent stretched out before me and having by then passed the huge racing fleet, the apparent lack of yachts at once looked wonderful – free space to sail. Clear water or not, on the bow, marking a transit to Portsmouth harbour entrance was the War Memorial and further inland a dramatic new addition to the skyline, the 170 metre high Spinnaker Tower. Just after 16:00 I started the engine and followed the small boat channel to enter this busy commercial port. Haslar Marina looked to be conveniently located so I steered Hobo into a vacant berth just behind the stomach churning Kermit green coloured redundant Light Ship which now serves the marina as a restaurant.

*10 August – Day 85. Gosport to Brighton. Passage 43 nm, 9:08 hours*

Haslar is just a short walk from Gosport High Street, happily well provided with cafés where that great sailors' breakfast of bacon and eggs can be enjoyed. With the prospect of a sunny day and a fair passage I ate heartily and thought of how this little part of Hampshire had, for centuries, seen legions of mariners arrive and recover their strength before departing once more for the sea. Although recently closed at the stroke of a pen by some forgettable Minister of Defence, Haslar, for more than 250 years, was the home to a hospital for Sailors of the Fleet and one can imagine the local Taverns and Inns once shaking to the sound of sea shanties and stories of sea battles.

Although real sea battles seem to be something the Royal Navy now avoids – consider the recent kidnapping episodes off Iraq and then Somalia – the pontoons of Haslar marina bore witness to the sailor's more traditional spirit of combat. With just two days before the start of the notorious Fastnet race, yachts and their crews were gathering. Stores were being loaded and sails and rigging being checked. The only thing missing from the Gosport scene was the polishing of cannon and muskets.

At 09:50 the tide and Hobo beckoned me and like so many mariners before, I steered my craft out into the harbour to catch the east going current. With the masts of Admiral Nelson's HMS Victory to my stern, Hobo turned to the southeast and on the bow met the huge grey shape of aircraft carrier HMS Illustrious, returning after unknown duties, far from the home waters. Added to these poignant reminders of Britain at war were the four now decaying huge concrete and iron sea forts, built in the 1860s to guard

Portsmouth against a possible invasion by our perennial old adversary, France. Happy indeed should this generation be, that now we have freed ourselves from the thousand year need to "rattle our sabres" at our neighbours. The sun shone brightly as I piloted a course between the forts and channel markers.

Since the sea conditions were good and the wind was in the south, my passage plan called for me to take the inside route around Selsey Bill and for this I needed to locate a green buoy named Boulder. From this mark I would then cross the shoals on a course of 090 degrees, until reaching East Borough Head cardinal. It took just over three hours to reach the buoy Boulder and from there I watched nervously both compass and echo sounder as Hobo tracked the 6 nautical miles to find deeper water. I believe it is perfectly reasonable to be a little nervous when sailing a deep fin keel yacht over a sand bank at a speed of nearly 6 knots.

This sand bank is far more than just sand, it is thought to be the site of Cymensora, where, in 477AD, the first Saxon invaders arrived to conquer the Britons – described by the Saxons as "welsh" – and settle the island so recently abandoned by the Roman legions. Over the centuries the sea engulfed the town of Cymensora and the shoals off Selsey Bill are the result. Happily, Hobo glided over this ancient history without incident.

At 14:35 I reached East Borough Head buoy and freed off the sheets allowing a course for Brighton. Soon after this the VHF radio interrupted my meditation with a Digital Selective Calling (DSC) distress call – in French. Regrettably I don't speak this language so I was unable to judge how serious the distress or the whereabouts of the caller. I sailed on. Brighton lay 22 nautical miles to the east.

To the north lay West Sussex with its towns of Littlehampton, Worthing, Shoreham-by-Sea and Hove.

Three hours passed as hours on a solo passage do, full of chart plotting, scouring the horizon and tea making.

Sailing towards a lee shore is psychologically uncomfortable. Something deep inside the mind, probably the inherited genetic memory of many thousands of long dead seafarers, creates unease. Boats don't have brakes and steering downwind towards a solid coast, complete with surf breaking on the beach, suggests to the mind "threat" rather than haven. One wants to see a bright sign – something marking a huge opening in the wall of surf saying "welcome". There rarely is one. At Brighton the only "sign" is very grey, very low and very difficult to see. At Brighton the welcome sign is a small opening between pieces of weathered concrete. To increase this particular sailor's stress, the sea off Brighton marina was confused. Waves and current bouncing back off the concrete threw Hobo around making arrival all the more tiring.

Nevertheless the chart showed an opening and the GPS chart plotter showed an opening, so a mariner has to trust and sail towards the hard shore. At 18:31 I spotted the entrance just east of the pier and, after a hurried drop of the sails, motored though the narrow gap into peace and an expensive surreal world of shiny moored craft. Brighton Marina wouldn't be out of place on the Cote d'Azur, but on this day I was more than happy that it was on my route to the Thames. At 18:58 Hobo was secure and I rewarded myself with a much needed meal at a busy marina restaurant.

*11 August – Day 86. Brighton to Eastbourne. Passage 22 nm, 4:25 hours*

The delights of Brighton town are undoubtedly well-known and it may not surprise readers that in the past Brighton "enjoyed" the attentions of our French neighbours, imbued with all their Gallic ideas of liberating England by fire. Only the area known as the Lanes survived the flambé and of course it is the Lanes which today provides much of the town's character and colour. However, a visit to the Lanes required a substantial walk from the gates of the marina, so instead I decided to rest and prepare for my next passage. Dover was the obvious destination but more than twelve and a half hours away so I decided to break the journey and investigate Eastbourne en route.

The weather forecast was of concern as there was a substantial low pressure system approaching from the west, I knew also that the three weeks of light breezes was soon to end. However, IF the forecast and pressure charts were correct I would have time to get to Eastbourne and perhaps Dover before gale force winds arrived.

At 07:17 I slipped the mooring lines, hopefully without waking too many of those around me, then motored Hobo out of the shiny "water world" that is Brighton Marina. Once more the sun shone but with the east breeze it felt more than a little cold.

Once outside the entrance I pointed Hobo to the southeast and tracked down the coast towards Beachy Head. Past Newhaven and Seaford the scenery improved and by 09:30 I had reached the dramatic white humps of the Seven Sisters, which stand like a fairy tale Ivory Castle besieged by the ocean. Yet these white walls are of chalk and from an organism far smaller than an elephant. It still amazes me that the chalk in these cliffs is the remains of countless billion of marine algae which lived when the sea level was at a height such as to cause today's proponents of global warming to foam at the mouth.

My turning point was south of the 162 metre high Beachy Head and its waterside "barber pole" painted light house. As I stared up at the cliff and the green meadow that stops abruptly at the edge, I could see several tiny figures taking their morning exercise and probably returning my gaze. I hoped they would stay there as Beachy Head seems to attract "jumpers" and the last thing I wanted was to witness a suicide. Happily for me – and the walkers – we remained far apart, they on the damp grass, and me on the water.

As the sea conditions were congenial, the flood tide caused barely a ripple in the water, yet still had the power to speed Hobo onward towards Eastbourne. A beach gradually came into view, complete with rows of guest houses and hotels. What with the summer sun and sparkling sea, I again thought of childhood holidays, ice creams and sandcastles. There is something of simple innocence about family holidays by the British seaside that no amount of Spanish heat or paella can match. Though Eastbourne still attracts the frivolous holiday crowd, I was a man with a mission yet to be completed.

To the East of the seafront lies Sovereign Harbour with its modern marina and housing development. A short breakwater and Martello Tower marks the entrance and after dropping the sails Hobo passed through the shallow muddy channel and was locked into the inner basin. At 11:42 the engine was silenced and I found myself with the unusual prospect of free time and the opportunity to explore.

Sovereign Harbour is a modern development designed to meet the need of Brits who want to have a house together with a berth for their boat. Sadly for boat owners, most of our natural harbours and estuaries are subject to the will of committees made up of well meaning "environmentalists", who are neither local nor friendly to the needs of humans. The bizarre restrictions whereby all sedimentary mud laid down over the past few hundred years is now "conserved", means our natural and historic liberty to use land with water access has been stolen. To law makers and lobbyists, the welfare of birds and worms is now considered more important than the health and mental wellbeing of local people or the jobs and commerce that has always funded the development of the nation. Of course the fundamental concept of protecting our natural heritage from reckless development is very laudable, but I ask why not return the estuaries and rivers to their beautiful condition before they became clogged and polluted by waste mud washed down from inland farmland? If the rivers were to be "conserved" in their original natural state they would be navigable once more and there would be ample room for waterside wharves and jetties where people could live and work.

As a consequence of having being denied use of much of the waterside land, Brits today have to resort to buying high-density, high-cost housing in neat new "brown field" marina developments like Sovereign. Oh well I'm sure Britain's worms are happy.

Efficient and convenient though Sovereign undoubtedly is, I wanted to experience a little more of the local character and with this in mind, I shouldered my rucksack and set out to walk along the promenade to the town.

From Sovereign, the beach with its raised Parade stretches like the Yellow Brick Road to the wizards of Eastbourne. Past the Martello Tower – one of the forts built to deter visits from our friends from France – I trekked, enjoying the view and the sunshine. After so many weeks of bleak grey weather and often glum little towns, Eastbourne Parade seemed to represent holidays and pleasure. Munchkin like children played in the shallows and adults with chilly pink bodies dumped on towels, absorbed vitamin D and ice cream. A fantasy land, and after so much isolation on my small yacht, I felt happy to have space to walk and share my day with so many of my fellow citizens. Painted beach huts, rows of bare wooden groynes, pink candy floss and the occasional lycra clad “rollerblade” skater, all helped create a carnival like atmosphere. Eastbourne is well worth a visit.

*12 August – Day 87. Eastbourne to Dover. Passage 45 nm, 8:05 hours*

The evening weather forecast showed the low pressure system still approaching along a line that would bring strong winds to the southeast coast, possibly later that night or the next. I believed I could reach Dover before the arrival of the gale and the fact that the wind, when it arrived would be from the southwest and that Dover offered all weather and all tide access, was reassuring. Despite the forecast I would sail. At 05:50 I had Hobo in the marina lock and soon Pevensey Bay and the glassy sea stretched out before me. It was here, off a sheltered beach at Pevensey on 28 September in 1066, the Norman fleet anchored and disembarked their warriors prior to settling a silly family quarrel. Like so many events of English history, war and misery for the many was caused by the failure of the few to plan succession. Had Edward, the so-called Confessor, better attended to family matters, any “conquest” would have been unnecessary.

On a course of 075 degrees I motored eastward, accompanied by two other yachts. The towns of Bexhill and Hastings were soon passed on the port beam. At just after 07:00, over the VHF radio Dover Coast Guard issued a strong wind warning. Wind was on its way but meanwhile the mainsail merely hung on its halyard. The hours passed. By 09:30 I was south of Rye and a light southerly breeze had arrived to improve my mood and provide motivation to move about the deck, pull sheets and gaze at the masthead wind indicator.

The turning point ahead was the headland of Dungeness

with its two nuclear power stations and perky lighthouse. Once round this corner I would be able to free the sheets and head for Dover. Nuclear power stations are strange things and on my circumnavigation I had passed quite a few. The writers and presenters of popular media portray these huge grey windowless buildings in such a manner that it is easy to imagine the devil himself resides within. On sailing by one, even a rational human like myself, tends to sense an inner anxiety, created perhaps by the relentless propaganda broadcast about this carbon neutral power source. However, local fishermen choose to cast their lines into the water at the "the boil", the place where the waste hot cooling water, fresh from the reactor, exits to the sea. Apparently fish and their prey welcome the contribution from the power station. I had visions of three eyed fish and, somewhere in the plant, a Monty Burns type boss laughing despotically; such is the power of media and of course the *Simpsons* cartoon. Luckily Hobo didn't encounter any mutant monsters or begin to glow in the dark, so I presume all is still well at Dungeness. At 10:45 I rounded the headland, altered course to 050 degrees and stared ahead, searching for Dover still 17 nautical miles away.

By 11 o'clock the breeze had strengthened, and with my mind focused on the weather forecast, I decided Dover was definitely "it", and although there would have been time to reach Ramsgate before nightfall, it wasn't prudent to push on. Several porpoise then joined me, they too heading northeast, and their presence helped lessen the feeling of isolation that often accompanies a solo sailor. I was now making fast progress.

Soon Folkestone was abeam and on the horizon I could see the repeated white shapes of cross channel ferries, arriving and leaving the port of Dover. At 13:30, while plotting my position on the chart, I realised Cap Gris Nez, on the French coast was a mere 17 nautical miles to the south. Dreams of fromage and chocolate croissant drifted through my mind but only for a second as the busy harbour entrance of Dover was now close. The pilot book told of the need to seek permission before entry and warned of a strong east bound current sweeping past the entrance. I needed to be active and concentrate. I didn't want to find myself under the bows of a France bound ferry or get swept past the harbour.

The current was indeed vicious, but at 13:50 I steered Hobo between the piers and headed towards Dover Marina, choosing a berth in the tidal harbour. At 14:15 and well away from all the ferries, with the engine silent and warps secure to a pontoon, I had a my second lunch of the day.

While I was happy to have arrived in Dover, I quickly found the reality of a town at the crossing point to the continent hard to endure. Dover was such a contrast with happy, neat Eastbourne. Dover appeared to me to have sacrificed its soul to the ferry business. The town and its harbour had been separated with the latter dominated by the roads leading to and from the ferry port. Whereas perhaps once travellers stayed several days at a local Tavern or Inn, spending money and awaiting fair weather or a convenient ship, today's traveller arrives by car a mere hour before scheduled departure and sees nothing of Dover, save the ugly large car park inside the terminal. To walk from the marina to anywhere in Dover was to endure exhaust fumes, dirt and crossing multi-lane carriageways, designed not for the ease of people, but to "corral" snorting vehicles into vicious never ending queues. I never did reach the town centre, so I turned myself toward the sea and explored the western breakwater. Here I found a different reality but one equally unexpected. I discovered scores of what I understood to be immigrant males "industrially" fishing from the Admiralty pier, apparently not for amusement, but with a fixed determination to haul in enough food for breakfast, lunch and dinner.

I felt I needed an early escape. With the low pressure system and its accompanying gale already beating the coast of the west country, I feared being harbour bound in Dover. I didn't want to spend the next few days in the maritime equivalent of a motorway underpass outside Heathrow airport. The question was, if the conditions were fine in the morning, would I have time to reach Ramsgate before the gale arrived?

*13 August – Day 88. Dover to Ramsgate. Passage 16 nm, 2:53 hours*

The dawn was offering a bright sky and southwesterly breeze so I took a walk to the pier to observe the sea conditions. It looked fine and I still had the annoying urge to leave. I didn't want to spend the next few days in transit camp Dover with Ramsgate a mere 16 nautical miles away. I returned to the boat and listened to the morning radio forecasts repeat what I already knew, there was a gale coming, probably soon. But my decision was made.

At 10:20, via the VHF radio I received permission to leave the marina and ten minutes later I was exiting the harbour. Once outside I found the wind was from the southwest and probably force 4 to 5, but it would soon be pushing Hobo downwind towards South Foreland. My theory was, as the wind was behind me, if it increased I could shorten sail and once around the next headland, safely pass along in the lee of the coast. Under working jib alone and assisted by the current, Hobo was skipping along at 7 knots over the ground.

While I checked the chart and traced my route with my finger, I suddenly had a hazy memory from my days at secondary school – a class of children and me singing at the top of my voice while the teacher bashed out a tune on a battered piano:

Farewell and adieu to you fair Spanish Ladies,
Farewell and adieu to you ladies of Spain;
For we've received orders for to sail for old England,
But we hope very soon we shall see you again.

Now the first land we made it is called the Dodman,
Next Rame Head off Plymouth, Start, Portland and Wight;
We sailed by Beachy, by Fairlee and Dungeness,
Until we came abreast of the South Foreland Light.

Little did I know then that I would one day sail the same course, although sadly not get the chance to meet or enjoy those fair Spanish Ladies.

By 11 o'clock I was indeed off South Foreland, and from there I could see across to the fabled Goodwin Sands off to the east. The Goodwins are the infamous set of banks that stretch in a 12 nautical mile line off the coast of Kent. Even Shakespeare had heard of them and in *The Merchant of Venice* he had an actor report of a wreck "where the carcasses of many a tall ship lie buried". I could see the warning buoys and the line of breaking waves thrown up by the combination of wind, currents and shoals. The Goodwins was a place I really didn't want to see from close up. Happily though my course had put the wind over the stern quarter and I was able inch the boat closer to the Kent shore.

By 11:50 I was off the town of Deal and as I rushed northward I met a fleet of racing yachts battling the other way. I was later to discover that this was the week of Ramsgate's annual regatta. However, at that moment, while

I admired the tenacity of the completing crews all taking a pounding as their yachts beat to windward, I had my own challenge. I was just 5 nautical miles from Ramsgate and approaching at a speed of about 8 knots. I started to realise I had three difficulties – lets not describe them as problems. Firstly the wind had increased and the entrance channel to Ramsgate required I turn Hobo on to a close reach. Secondly, there was just the single narrow harbour entrance with tide sweeping across rather than into the harbour. Lastly, when I radioed for permission to enter, the Harbour control instructed me to "wait". To wait outside would have been to add two or three additional problems to my list.

With Hobo over pressed by the increasing wind and being swept north by the tide I could not wait and risk missing the entrance. I believed if I didn't achieve the harbour on my first attempt I would not have been able to fight back against both wind and current. Also, I knew the undersized and continually "sick" Volvo diesel didn't have enough power for me to return directly against the rising wind. To miss the harbour entrance on my first attempt would mean Hobo would probably be driven past Ramsgate and out off North Foreland and the outer Thames Estuary. This would not be good.

I knew I had a one time opportunity to make the entrance and neither wind or tide allowed me to wait. So I disregarded the Harbour Control instruction and steered Hobo up tide and up wind of the entrance. Dropping the jib wasn't really an option as I didn't believe the engine had enough power to ensure I could keep my course. I'm sure my arrival in Ramsgate harbour entertained a few people on the breakwater and annoyed those officials watching the radar screen. Hobo still under sail, shot through the entrance to the ferry harbour like an arrow through a castle window. Here I quickly turned her into wind and let go the halyard. Once the jib had been tied down I ran aft and steered Hobo into the Royal Harbour and between the rows of pontoons. There was a little more excitement still to come, but happily a friendly German sailor noticed I was sailing solo and came to my aid as the cross wind propelled Hobo, a little less than delicately, into a vacant berth. At 13:08 it was all over, I had made it. Ramsgate looked really wonderful.

A little later I checked the wind readings and realised it had been force 7 as I had entered the harbour. Lunch followed and I watched a continual stream of wounded racing yachts creep back into the marina having abandoned the competition due to breakages of various kinds.

*14 – 15 August. Days 89 – 90. Ramsgate*

Unfortunately Hobo was not wholly unscathed following the brisk wind conditions off Ramsgate. The hard working jib that, with the mainsail, had pulled Hobo around Britain, suffered a split seam and it needed to be repaired before putting to sea again. Happily on the harbour side in Ramsgate I found a cooperative sail loft and they promised the jib would be ready in 24 hours.

What with the gale bouncing and shaking all the boats in the harbour, a delay for a sail repair wasn't really a problem. So I relaxed and allowed myself to explore and enjoy Ramsgate.

This was my first visit to the town and I can recommend the place to all those who might regard the English seaside as "boring". Ramsgate has a beach, a Royal harbour, pleasant architecture and history. For instance, I didn't know it was on this spot that the Romans chose for their first settlement back around 40AD and it was here in the year 597 a certain monk called Augustine, when he was still plain Signor, began his conversion of the Sassenach Britons. Yet more historical "local gold" and fodder for the sober harbour bound sailor was the discovery that it was here around the year 449 that a pair of sausage eating Saxons, the brothers Hengist and Horsa, began their bloody bid for an fourth-century version of *X Factor*. Ramsgate has so much hard-core history I puzzled over why, when I was a schoolboy, no teacher thought to bring me here on an educational visit.

My other significant epiphany that day was the understanding that, if I had been sailing Hobo back in 40AD, I could have sailed right around Ramsgate, it being then on the offshore Isle of Thanet and separated from Kent by the salty Wantsum Channel. Think here of the Isle of Sheppey or Canvey, but with Roman legions in leather skirts and sandals collecting shells on the beach. It was the fact that Thanet was a safe island off the mainland that attracted Romans, Saxons and Augustine. Rather than any currently fashionable fuzzy climatic theory, the archaeological evidence of a Roman harbour two miles inland from the coast, perhaps suggests that the sea level in 40AD was higher than today. So a relaxing day for me and, if it had not been for my habitual concern for the weather, I would truly have been at peace.

On Wednesday morning the wind still blew, so much so, that I was entertained for a couple of hours by the struggles of a large car ferry blown aground across the harbour entrance. Nothing could leave or arrive while the embarrassed captain trashed his engines trying to free the ship. This was just one of the factors which encouraged me to seek out the train departures for London. A brief trip home seemed sensible. London was so close and I could open my mail, water my plants and use the washing machine. It was too tempting to resist so I locked up Hobo and, with a rucksack on my back, headed home for one night.

The TV weather forecasts suggested the low pressure system that had brought the gale to our south coast was soon safely past and probably on its way to annoy the happy Volvo driving, herring eaters of Scandinavia. The wind looked fair for a passage and I returned by train to Hobo late Thursday evening.

*17 August – Day 91. Ramsgate to Chatham. Passage 52 nm, 10:13 hours*

The Imray navigation chart for the outer Thames estuary offers an image not unlike a bad piece of lottery funded art. Lots of wiggly shady bits on pale blue, without form or pattern. Each shady bit is a sand shoal, each in turn providing another metaphorical dog turd on the pathway of a sailor hoping to reach London. The passage homeward was going to be more complicated than I had imagined and I realised why, over the millennia, many invaders chose to land in Kent and walk their way west rather than face the obstacles of the Thames estuary. However, there was a route through and the friendly people of Trinity House had littered the channels with a scattering of red and green cans and numerous painted cardinal buoys, bobbing on the water like so many floating giant wasps. All I had to do was choose a route and then find and closely follow the markers. It may sound easy but when the tidal current, wind and waves are added into the equation there were a lot of variables.

My plan was to leave Ramsgate four hours after high water Dover, butt the foul current as I sailed north and then turn west, allowing the, by then, in-rushing, rising tide to whoosh Hobo safely over the shallows towards the Medway and Chatham. On paper it looked a fine plan.

At 06:15 I saluted a sunny morning and the light

southwesterly breeze. I quickly exited Ramsgate harbour and set sail on a close reach towards North Foreland headland. As is so often the case with the major turning points around our coastline, this rocky headland needed to be served with an ASBO as it was having such a bad influence on the wind. The wind suddenly blew strongly and Hobo swayed, showing a lot of bottom. Within minutes I had to put two reefs in the mainsail to allow Hobo to recover her dignity. Despite the contrary current, she was making 4 knots over the ground, healthy enough and well within my expectations. By 07:38 I was abeam Longnose Point and about a mile offshore. It was at this juncture I could have turned due west and closely followed the north Kent coast, that is, if I had been sailing something without nearly two metres of iron and GRP beneath the water line. The seemingly attractive channel just offshore of Margate peters out after 7 miles and, from that point on, it would have been a scary keel scraping and horrid passage to the Medway. Probably possible but certainly full of risks. My choice was to take the longer but safer route north to Princes channel.

According to my reading of the tidal charts, by the time I left the north Kent coast the contrary tidal stream should have slackened and perhaps even swung in my favour. Either the tidal chart was wrong or I was wrong, the current didn't slacken. This was frustrating as it meant my passage plan underestimated the time needed to reach the Medway. It was going to be a long day.

Once well away from North Foreland the wind eased down and I shook out one reef, followed by the second an hour later. With the wind then from the west, Hobo was close hauled and slowed by the tidal current heading out to the north sea. At 09:21 Hobo reached the Outer Princes cardinal, the second of a spotty rash of buoys that would mark the various shoals and channels scattered across, what an innocent sailor could have hoped to be, a clear wide expanse of water. I then had to beat against the wind up the Princes Channel between the Shingles and Ridge Tongue sand banks.

The process required for each and every tack was this; watch the water depth reading on the echo sounder display decrease until it showed just 2.5 metres and then tack the boat by pushing the tiller away, free off the leeward jib sheet, pirouetting my body around to face the opposite direction, pulling the tiller to amidships while, at the same time, hauling in the new leeward jib sheet. Then a few cranks on the sheet winch to trim the jib and again watch the depth on the echo sounder display until it decreased once more as I approached the opposite side of the liquid alleyway. The whole process was repeated and repeated – such is sailing to windward up a narrow channel between sand banks. Later that day, after I had arrived at Chatham, I checked the GPS chart plotter memory for detail of my track from Outer Princes buoy. To beat through all the channels and sand banks of the estuary I had completed forty-eight tacks – solo.

At last at 10:20, halfway along Princes Channel, I noticed the water current had changed in my favour. From this point, the nature of this planet with its distant moon would lend a hand. Hobo would be "lifted" forward rather than pulled back. This divine assistance helped cheer my mood, as by then, I'd realised I still had at lot of tacking to face.

At 11:26 I was abeam Princes 7 cardinal buoy and able to pass into the mysteriously named Knob channel. Dead ahead of Hobo lay the rusting and rotting eyesores that are the Shivering Sands Towers. This remnant of World War II defences is one of the four surviving sets of the original seven forts built in the Thames estuary. If anyone believes the seemingly pro-environmental rhetoric, mouthed by various ministers of the UK government, let them look on this abandoned waste metal left for sixty-five years to decay and mar the natural seascape. Any responsible Government truly valuing our Island, having noticed that World War II was over, would surely have had the redundant junk removed. Instead, the sand banks of the Thames estuary will soon have a number of new man made constructions – more wind turbines. The media report the London Array will one day have 341 giant turbines planted in concrete structures resting on the sea bed. One could speculate on the destiny of these new installations and, perhaps, imagine we were trying to sail these waters in a hundred years hence. Lest we doubt the ultimate fate of offshore turbines, once a future Government decides to abandon public subsidy, we could just look at the junk left on today's aptly named Shivering Sands.

Knob Channel joined Knock John Channel – just who were those people immortalised on these marine charts? – and my physical work-out continued. Tack, then another tack – dodge a ship – tack. It was hard work but I felt energised that I was now in home waters. After eighty-nine days away I was once again sailing the sediment filled grey water that sluiced, twice in every twenty-four hours, all the way up to the Pool of London. It seemed to me hard to believe that this was indeed the outer reaches of the Thames. Smile though I did, I still knew that I had one more new experience ahead before, perhaps in a couple of days, at Gravesend I would pass familiar river banks.

I sailed past Red Sands Towers and pointed Hobo's bow at the 244 metre high chimney of the power station that marks the west side of the entrance to the Medway. With the wind still from west southwest, I had many more tacks to complete and what with this and the need to avoid the line of ships both arriving and leaving the Thames, I was up and down more often than a honeymoon couple. More channel buoys slipped satisfyingly by, Ooze, East Cant, Medway and err No 2 – clearly someone naming the buoys had run out of inspiration at this point. I had now entered the relatively narrow shipping channel leading to the Medway and soon, off my starboard bow, I saw the warning marks and telltale masts of the wreck of the USS Montgomery. This ship sank here in August 1944 and the records suggest there are still 3,000 tons of munitions and explosives in its hold. An interesting fact to ponder on as you are forced to sail within twenty metres of what could now be thought of as a huge IED. The theory offered by the pilot book is that the ship's explosive cargo is considered too dangerous to remove. Just what sort of hole in the sea 3,000 tons of sixty-five year old explosive could make I don't know but I didn't like being close enough to care.

At this point the tide rushing into the Medway carried Hobo forward and I sailed holding to the Garrison Point side of the entrance. At 14:11 Hobo was abeam of the Fort at Garrison and a new estuary opened before me. As this was my first time in the Medway I decided it would be prudent to drop the sails and proceed on under engine. Here again the wonderful little glowing screen of the GPS chart plotter proved itself worth a "fist full of dollars", showing the best way forward and allowing me to avoid taking a wrong turn – and there are a lot of "dead end" creeks on the Medway.

The north shore is dominated by the Isle of Grain power station, a busy container port and several redundant piers and jetties. No longer an island and bereft of any grain, it seems the dubious fun of electricity generation now dominates the economy and landscape. All fairly grim sights unless, I suppose, your wage packet colours the view. To the south lies a confusing mass of marsh, doubtless full of privileged happy worms and attendant itinerant wild fowl. I understand that in warmer times the marsh even provided malaria as a free souvenir for locals and visitors alike. The main river channel wanders to the southwest past the Kingsnorth Power station and Darnett Ness Fort. Lest for a moment we forget the nation's almost constant state of war, Hoo Fort provides the necessary reminder. Then the town of Gillingham is on the bow and increasing numbers of small boat moorings confirm my version of civilisation is indeed near. I had decided to berth Hobo at Chatham Marina in the old naval dockyard and this required that I pass further on up the river. Soon the masts and flags signified a harbour and I locked into the basin. It had taken a full two hours to travel from Garrison point to Chatham but at 16:28 Hobo and I were resting alongside a pontoon.

*18 August – Day 92. Chatham*

I had chosen to sail past Gillingham and on to Chatham because of the latter's past not its present. The marina is sited in the Royal Dockyard that, from the time of Elizabeth I, re-supplied brave seaman such Drake and Hawkins and helped in the preparations to defend England from the Spanish Armada. Over the dockyard's 400 year history more than 500 ships were built and, at its height, as many as 10,000 workers found employment. It was here Admiral Nelson's flagship HMS Victory – still in good condition at Portsmouth – was built in 1765. While the drama was once great so was the stage. Three huge flooded basins, complete with five dry docks, were dug out of the mud and lined with brick and stone. The place is a testament to British workers, great civil engineering and enterprise.

Chauffeur driven politicians closed this manufacturing dockyard in 1984. Times change of course, although the need for commerce and healthy employment does not.

The dockyard resource bequeathed to the nation by all the craftsmen and workers who toiled here for 400 years could have been utilised for new marine industry – perhaps even for building the structures or turbines for the proposed London Array. But no, it seems that along with integrity, our politicians have lost the ability to be visionary. Today's dockyard is nearly deserted and home to just two equally trivial manifestations of a society that consumes but now doesn't manufacture. Today's trump card to 400 years of enterprise and engineering is the Dockside Outlet Centre and Dickens World. Just how low can a nation sink? I was glad I had chosen Chatham Marina but was saddened by the fate of the once glorious dockyard.

*19 August – Day 93. Chatham to Erith. Passage 38 nm, 7:36 hours*

London was calling me and, despite having seen only a fraction of the Medway Estuary, I felt an impatience to finish my voyage. In ten days time I had to be back at work and although only one day away from home, there would be several days of clearing up before I would be able to say farewell to Hobo.

My plan for the day was to take the last two hours of ebb tide out to the river mouth and then use the ingoing flood to sweep Hobo up the Thames. So it was another early start and at 07:44 I locked out of the marina and joined the Medway as it meandered between the moorings and mud banks. The view ahead seemed familiar but perhaps by this point in my adventure, both water and sky combined as if in a painting by Joseph Turner, and the swirl of light somehow beckoned me forward. Down the Medway River heading once more for the sea and as I passed along, I tried to pick out, with the binoculars, the strange steeple of Upchurch. For it was here one Edmund Drake, father of young Francis, was a parish priest for seven years until his death in 1567. Edmund, from the year 1549, had been a Medway resident and the story is told that young Francis joined his father, the two of them living together in an old abandoned hulk through the hard times. Francis saw what I saw but whereas I sailed for amusement, he was apprenticed to a local ship owner and learned true seamanship, transporting trading goods along the Kent coast and on to the Low Countries to the east.

As I passed the muddy entrance to Half Acre Creek and continued out toward the Thames, I thought of a young Francis taking the same route more than 400 years before. Often this thing we call time has no meaning.

At 09:45 I was abeam Garrison Point and turned Hobo towards the Nore Swatch buoy and the distant Canvey Island. The now unused anchorage of the Nore lay to starboard, once temporary home to so many Men-O-War during the "sporting series" of the Anglo-Dutch wars – no not the French this time. The huge Thames Estuary had at last narrowed, allowing me to sense that this was indeed the mouth of a river rather than just a curve in the coastline. Of course the wind exhaled straight from London – I could almost smell the traffic – and I smiled to think there would be yet more tacking today. I could see the urban sprawl of Southend-on-Sea teetering on the north shore, merging gradually into Leigh-on-Sea and thought how it seemed to me both towns had turned their faces away from the less salubrious vista of silver storage tanks and massed pipes that make up the huge Oil Refinery at Shellhaven. Coming home to the Thames, one sees little of this island's natural beauty, just the now normal scarred habitat of massed homo sapiens.

By 12:30 I had passed the creek at Holehaven and the muddy river banks gradually closed in as the sea yielded up its identity in the face of abuse that has lasted as long as man's settlement. Grandeur there is none, just a sense that the river leads somewhere dangerous – like a well trodden pathway through a waste tip. The navigational chart offers nothing encouraging. There is Lower Hope Reach with its Mucking Flats, Coalhouse Point and the first town on the Thames, Gravesend – names all together suggesting something of the psyche of the lower river.

A traveller might imagine that the first and last port on a river which serves as a watery highway to a capital city, of a once great empire, would offer a dramatic welcome. Perhaps well maintained visitor pontoons, an efficient marina or a picturesque sheltered harbour? One could imagine national flags and a little visual pomp and ceremony. Alas, here on the lower Thames there is nothing to suggest that Britain has pride in herself or that she graciously greets visitors or welcomes home her citizens. Commercial shipping might be met by a pilot boat or harbour master and then escorted to Tilbury docks or to those giant yellow buoys provided by the Port of London Authority, but all leisure yachts are shunned and treated with cruel contempt. After a long passage through the hazardous sand banks of the estuary, a visitor to the Thames from a distant foreign land has little choice but to sail on by Gravesend, the river side appearing to be quite hostile to small craft and their crews. While there is the stately Victorian Town Pier, this is closed to leisure craft and there are no public pontoons or jetties, waterside pubs or restaurants where a small boat could stop. It will be another 30 miles or more before a visitor has any chance of finding a safe berth or being able to place their feet on "England's green and pleasant land".

From Gravesend Reach the river winds past Tilbury Docks and the private boat moorings off Thurrock Yacht Club. Next comes ancient Greenhithe, on a broad bend in the river, surely a perfect location for a yacht harbour? The Romans and the Saxons both recognised the potential. Surely someone in the present day British government, perhaps with pride in the nation, or even the Port of London Authority could at last recognise the needs of international visitors arriving in small boats? Perhaps ironically, the area has even been designated as the Thames Gateway but of course for the planners this gateway is for road vehicles and commuters not mariners.

The Queen Elizabeth II Bridge as a portent of things to come, contributes both traffic fumes and road noise and I was very relieved to pass under and upwind of this busy roadway. Noises off the river compete with one another. On Long Reach the rather unnerving sound of racing motor bike engines and occasional blasts from shotguns suggest the local natives of Dartford prefer their nature shattered, dead or with tyre tracks. Even more unpleasant signals of land use are carried on the wind. As I approached Crayford Ness the smell of London's decaying rubbish wafted across from the Coldharbour terminal and the adjacent Aveley Marshes. The lower Thames is like the hidden dirty back alley to the kitchens of an expensive city restaurant.

Despite being no more than three hours from Limehouse marina I chose to break the passage with one last night on the water. Erith Yacht Club squats on the mud between a yard full of rubbish skips and some old run down wharves. Nonetheless the club members are very friendly and efficient at laying yacht moorings. On one of their vacant buoys, at the far end of a trot, at 15:21 I moored Hobo and settled down to watch the river and the evening.

Regrettably the weather changed and the hoped for setting sun was hidden by grey damp clouds. Drizzle soon arrived and I was forced from the cockpit to shelter in the closed space of the cabin. The wash from Harbour Master launches and the tugs owned by Cory, towing lighters full of yet more stinking rubbish, meant Hobo rocked and shook herself all night. This was not the home coming I had allowed myself to imagine. This was a reawakening as to why I had left on my adventure in the first place.

*20 August – Day 94. Erith to Greenwich. Passage 14 nm, 3:18 hours*

Following a disturbed night I busied myself cleaning Hobo and emptying several of the below bunk lockers. Things I had misplaced weeks before at last came to hand, along with salt water and that curse of small boats, human hair. I think all mariners should be waterproof and bald – I failed in this basic genetic specification.

At 12:20 I slipped Hobo from the mooring buoy and like many hundreds of thousands of mariners over the centuries, I took the incoming flood tide up river towards London and the end of my voyage. A light westerly breeze ensured that I had to beat into the cold damp drizzle. When the wind is from the west it seems to follow every curve of the river ensuring, whatever the compass bearing, a boat heading for London is always close hauled. Erith Reach opened out into Halfway Reach with its potent Victorian sewage pumping station and its modern equivalent, a building all shiny and bold on the outside but inside full of the same type of stinking stuff. And on past Dagenham car plant complete with its fig leaves of twin wind turbines. If it wasn't the prospect of a glorious end, I'm sure no one would choose to endure the grim vista offered at every turn. To arrive in London by sea a mariner has to endure sights fit only for those who have given up on their fellow citizens and abandoned hope. It seems we are a nation post-imperial, post-industrial and more importantly post-pride.

Woolwich is the first sign after Gravesend that a different

England might just exist. While the tower blocks and apartments hardly represent beauty, the buildings suggest that at least here there is healthy life and homes for people. Even the Woolwich ferries shuttling back and forth like two giant woodlice allow a mariner to glimpse natives, in motion and living happily by this great waterway. I suddenly felt less alone.

At 13:55 I called up London VTS on the VHF radio to gain permission to pass through the Thames Barrier, a type of modern portcullis in the defences of London. Not far now and a childish excitement lifted my mood. I passed the converted and recycled crane platform that is now home to Greenwich Yacht Club. Ahead I could see the high-rise glass and steel towers which house the flawed financial wizards of Canary Wharf and also that white plastic monument to contemporary bad taste, The Millennium Dome. I could sense London's pulse, the current like vibration generated by eleven million people.

Eventually, over on the south bank, I reached those great maritime symbols of a different Britain, the Britain that celebrated achievement rather than just laid waste the land. Sir Christopher Wren's wonderful Greenwich Hospital, the Greenwich Observatory and Sir George Airy's Prime Meridian line are perhaps the only signs on thirty miles of the lower Thames, that suggest the inhabitants of this shrinking septre'd isle are anything other than brutish and blind to all beauty. Gazing from the river at Greenwich Hospital and from there to the Observatory one at last sees grandeur and symbols worthy of a great city. And this was it – my finish line. I had at last completed my circumnavigation adventure of this Island I call home – Greenwich to Greenwich.

# *Epilogue*

My ninety-four day travel adventure had ended but, of course, although there were no more charts to study or weather forecasts to decode, harbours to find or headlands to round, my personal journey would continue. I had visited the seas and coast of my "home" Islands and met the shore dwelling natives. These Scots, Ulster folk, Irish, Welsh and English islanders were mostly descended from the various invaders who chose to sail their boats here over the centuries. Perhaps surprisingly, I met very few of Britain's more recent immigrants, those having arrived by plane – perhaps they feel little spiritual connection to our sea and choose to live inland in the dry grey urban sprawl. I had seen for myself how the coastal people of our four nations, once as united as any extended family, are now embracing stories larded with nascent nationalism which will cause tears and may, one day, lead to estrangement. While saddened by the result of modern politics I felt excited by the discovery of so many beautiful places that are ours and still free for our collective enjoyment.

On stepping ashore for the last time I felt very satisfied and happy but it was a private, personal happiness I was somehow then unable to really share. No-one but me had benefited from my journey, yet I hope the wiser me that returned might now be a better man. I said my goodbyes to the beautiful Hobo and walked home where, once more, I became the anonymous urbane commuter on London's Jubilee line.

*"This Scepter'd Isle"*

This royal throne of kings, this scepter'd isle,
This earth of majesty, this seat of Mars,
This other Eden, demi-paradise,
This fortress built by Nature for herself Against infection and the hand of war,
This happy breed of men, this little world,
This precious stone set in the silver sea, which serves it in the office of a wall, or as a moat defensive to a house, against the envy of less happier lands,
This blessed plot, this earth, this realm, this [Britain]

*Richard II*, Act 2. Scene I.
William Shakespeare – 1595

## *Glossary*

**Abeam** – Right angles from the side of the boat.

**Autohelm** – Electronic device able to steer a yacht.

**Beat/beating** – Wind from directly in front. Sailing towards the wind by tacking the boat.

**Bow** – Front of the boat.

**Buoy** – Plastic or steel floating marker or mooring point.

**Chart** – Paper map of the sea area.

**Close hauled** – Sailing as close to the wind direction as possible.

**Ebb** – Out bound falling tidal current.

**Flood** – In bound rising tidal current.

**GPS chart plotter** – Type of Satnav for boats but without the annoying voice directions.

**Gybe** – Sailing downwind and steering to move the wind from one stern quarter to the other.

**Halyard** – Rope used to pull sail to the top of the mast.

**Knot** – A speed of one nautical mile per hour.

**Jib** – Small front sail.

**NM** – Nautical Miles i.e. 1 minute of latitude or 1852 metres equivalent to 1.150779 miles.

**Over falls** – A place where tidal currents push up over an obstruction and disturb the surface water.

**Race** – A place where tidal currents combine.

**Reach** – Wind from the side of the boat.

**Run** – Wind from directly behind the boat.

**Sheet** – Rope used to trim the sail to best use the wind.

**Stern** – Back of the boat.

**Tack/tacking** – Changing direction on a beat. Zig-zagging towards the wind.

**VHF** – Marine band two-way radio.

**Warps** – Rope used for mooring a boat.

# Appendix

## Statistics from around Britain Cruise

Total distance around Britain was 1900 nm
I visited 46 ports/anchorages
I was on board for 94 days
My average speed was 4.85 knots
1248 nm were sailed solo and 652 nm with crew

## Caledonian Canal – Timings between key points

| | |
|---|---|
| Clachnaharry sea lock to Seaport marina | 1:13 |
| Seaport marina to Dochgarroch | 3:10 |
| Dochgarroch to Fort Augustus (top lock) | 7:10 |
| Fort Augustus to Aberchalder swing bridge | 1:41 |
| Aberchalder swing bridge to Laggan swing bridge | 1:00 |
| Laggan swing bridge to Laggan lock | :50 |
| Laggan lock to Gairlochy 1:13 hours | 1:43 |
| Gairlochy to Banavie | 1:14 |
| Banavie to Corpach sea lock | 1:54 |
| Total passage time | 19:55 hours/mins |

## Navigation Charts

The minimum number of Imray charts needed to sail Greenwich to Greenwich is 18. Cost per chart (2007) £15.95.

**C2** The River Thames
**C1** Thames Estuary
**C29** Harwich to Whitby
**C24** Flamborough Head to Fife Ness
**C23** Fife Ness to Moray Firth
**C65** Crinan to Mallaig and Barra
**C63** Firth of Clyde
**C62** Irish Sea
**C61** St George's Channel
**C60** Gower Peninsula to Cardigan
**C58** Trevose Head to Bull Point
**C7** Falmouth, Isles of Scilly and Newquay
**C6** Salcombe to Lizard Point
**C5** Bill of Portland to Salcombe Harbour
**C4** Needles Channel to Bill of Portland
**C3** Isle of Wight
**C9** Beachy Head to the Isle of Wight
**C8** Dover Strait

## *Index*